THE GREAT WINE GRAPES

The Great Wine Grapes

and The Wines They Make

A Limited First Edition

The Great Wine Grapes

and The Wines They Make

by

Bern C. Ramey

with

Viticultural Profiles by Dr. Lloyd A. Lider,
Professor of Viticulture & Enology;
University of California
Davis, California

Photography by Timothy B. Ramey

R14

Library of Congress Cataloging in Publication Data
    Ramey, Bern C., 1919—
        The Great Wine Grapes: and The Wines They Make

Printed in the United States of America.

3218

Reader please note: You will find several areas in this book where double blank pages occur. This is necessary —simply because we do not want to deface the beauty of the elegant color photographs by printing on the reverse side. After research with this 80 pound vellum paper stock used throughout the book, the ink does show through, however slightly, on the photograph itself. (You may wish to frame some of these rare photographs).

Preface

The moral of this book is that you can't make a silk purse from a sow's ear, in this country or in any other wine-producing areas.

As the text clearly points out, it has taken the California grape and wine industry nearly forty years to recognize this. But, to their credit, they now understand it: it is the distinguishing earmark of the 1960's and 1970's in California and elsewhere. Today there are nearly 200,000 acres of newly-planted fine wine grapes in this state. Other wine-producing areas likewise have large plantings of recommended varieties.

This book will be a very useful guide to these "great" grapes: producers and consumers will find it equally illuminating. To understand California (or any other) wines one must understand their grapes. Here are the most important grape varieties: start here if you would understand one important reason why the quality of our California wines has improved so dramatically the last 15 years, and will continue to improve in the future.

Maynard A. Amerine
Professor of Enology, Emeritus,
University of California,
Davis, California

July 25, 1977

Introduction

It would be presumptuous of anyone to claim total understanding of America's relatively new-born enthusiasm for wine. It seems to be something that just "happened," as natural as fermentation itself. It was more of a renaissance, a re-discovery of the gentleness and refinement which make wine unique among all beverages. Europeans inherit this affection from their ancestors; Americans had to break through myth and misconception and have learned about wine's intrinsic values by first-hand experience.

Wine has become an object of study for the simple reason that it exists in such staggering diversity. Thus, along with this renewed interest, scores of volumes discussing wines from various countries have been generated. By and large the extant wine literature has focused on history, from general cultural studies to individual profiles of winegrowing estates and winemakers. More recently, the literature has become more esoteric in nature, looking at the soils and climates of specific regions and discussing the virtues of various vintages and particular wines. Each study adds something to our understanding of wine. Yet it seemed strange that the source or starting point of all these vinous treasures—the grape—remained largely ignored. How could one fully appreciate and enjoy wine without knowing more about the rudimentary "personalities" of the vine and its fruit? Wine appreciation ran head-on into this void, this large gap. Out of this essential question and the obvious need came the idea for _The Great Wine Grapes_.

What emerged in final form is something of a tightrope walker: not a technical, scientific treatise, but a basic and complete introduction to each grape variety's characteristics. Nor is this a collection of legends and anecdotes, though it includes the all-important traditions and histories of the varieties, as well as some personal indications about the various wines produced by each. This book is designed for anyone, whether novice or expert, who simply has a thirst for better understanding and appreciation of wine's myriad pleasures.

Behind this book is an ever-growing enthusiasm for what is called "varietal nomenclature." This labeling system by which certain wines meeting minimum standards may take the name of the predominant grape used is the definite wave of the future. Over the last few decades, there has been a dramatic increase in varietal labeling of wines in America, and its success is testified to by the way Europeans and winegrowers in other countries have adopted this system, mostly for export to this country. It has often shifted the emphasis from place or region to the grape variety grown there. By bringing us closer to the source, it has led to a real increase in precision, simplicity and, occassionally, I'm sure, greater honesty.

We have confined ourselves to the two of the species of the genus _Vitis_ which are cultivated by winegrowers today: the _Vitis labrusca_, native to North America and grown almost exclusively in vineyards east of the Rocky Mountains, and the _Vitis vinifera_, the prestigious European or Old World species of _Euvitis_ which has been successfully transplanted to the western United States and elsewhere. Most of the grape varieties belonging to these two species are familiar to American wine lovers.

But the stickiest problem of all was how to define the "great" wine grapes within each species. Ampelographers and grape breeders tell us there are more than 8,000 commercial varieties cultivated. Mercifully, one might add, hundreds of years of field studies and trial winemaking experiments have led viticulturalists and enologists to agree there are a few dozen varieties capable of yielding truly superior wines, and perhaps another few dozen which regularly produce wines of general appeal.

In any case, three essential conditions must be met for the making of a fine wine, with the first being a high-quality grape variety. That is, the grape must be able to develop at maturity the optimum sugar-to-acid ratio needed for a balanced wine. Secondly, the vine must be planted under climatic and soil conditions conducive to the development of fully-ripened grapes. Third, of course, is a devoted winemaker to whom material gain is subordinated to a quest for perfection. No winemaker, however, can alter the fact that one can never make truly fine wine from inferior grapes.

Once having said this, I can realize a quick glance at the table of contents may startle a few readers. If not by the inclusion of the Mission variety, then surely by the presence of the Aligoté,

Grey Riesling, Sylvaner, and the Concord, Delaware, Catawba trio. Personally, I'd rather risk seeming sacriligous in order to broaden the meaning of varietal greatness. The Cabernet Sauvignon, Chardonnay, and the White Riesling are great—in the classical sense. But isn't it sensible to include under "great" those varieties that excel in producing clean, pleasant wines in abundant quality at inexpensive prices? Are the workhorses and backbones of various wine cultures less important to the enjoyment of wine than the bluebloods and noble varieties? Or, as in the case of the Mission grape and the Concord family, could we possibly exclude these pioneering vines which spearheaded viticultural efforts in what was to emerge eventually as an important winegrowing country? When placed within historical perspective, these grapes have a special form of greatness conferred upon them. Thus, it seemed a little snobbish to ignore this type of grape by adhering too closely to traditional rigidities. Without these often maligned, always excluded lesser grape varieties, there simply would be no wine culture as we know it today.

Like any ongoing story, the saga of the grape has its heroes. But in this modern era it is no longer enough to offer the expected salutes to the European vintners who provided the rest of the world with standards and with painstakingly effective techniques. The reason is the emergence of a new force to be reckoned with, one which is no longer overshadowed or beholding to the European efforts. It includes more than a different and unique climate, some new hybrid varieties, or greater efficiency in production. It's all these elements drawn together by a new feeling, a new ethos in winemaking.

California vintners have at last established a worldwide reputation. The wines aren't just good; they are excellent by any standards. This reality is now accepted by the most skeptical connoisseur and wine critic. The "New Breed" of winemakers, a group which incidentally contains a fair share of women, has meshed together two powerful factors—science and art. One only needs to talk to them briefly to sense the dedication, enthusiasm, critical appreciation, and restless quest for perfection, all of which makes a job into a life's obsession.

Yet at the same time, there's always evidence of the cool, calculating head, the Yankee technician at work, in search of improved methods and a more precise understanding of all winemaking variables. In California we have a real resolution of opposites: the person courageous enough to shed any useless tradition, and sensible enough to continue a worthwhile, if laborious tradition . . . a vintner able to keep a careful eye on the delicate day-to-day operations, and still spin little daydreams which may ultimately manifest themselves in future glories. The wedding of these two inherently American tendencies has provided the energy for a quantum leap in wine quality and quantity, and what the fulfillment of present potential will be is anyone's pleasant guess.

The world of wine, united by a marvelous spirit of sharing and friendliness, is anything but static. It continues to revolve rapidly, well-oiled by an abundance of experimentation which propels it along toward new discoveries and changes. In this context, I'm reminded of an incident involving the late truly great wine expert, and a very good friend, Frank Schoonmaker. When a woman upon meeting him asked if he weren't "the man who knows everything about wine?" he replied kindly, "Madam, if that were true yesterday, it certainly is not true today." This book proceeds from that pragmatic, honest self-assessment.

The aim of this book is directed toward one of the more fragile but necessary human desires—appreciation of an art form. As such, wine is perhaps the most democratic of all aesthetic achievements. From my life-long involvement with wine, my experience has been that if one takes the time to develop an honest sensetivity to a beautiful thing, the rewards of that intimacy are vast and varied. Neither sentimental nor maudlin, the experience always leads to a discovery of something vital, life-giving, and life-enhancing. With wine, the sum of these personal adventures always seems to yield up that most singular moment of recognition: that out of all the myriad possibilities of creation, this multi-faceted fruit known as a grape should have been given to us at all. With deference to Ben Franklin, I have been convinced that a little grape is proof that God loves us. It behooves us all to become better acquainted with such gifts.

Acknowledgments

Whatever virtues this book possesses are due in large part to the wise counsel and gracious assistance of a number of old and dear friends. Some thirty-odd years ago, when I first began taking more than a layman's interest in wines and grape varities, I had the great good fortune of falling into the hands of the best possible guides. One should indeed be counted among the ungrateful if he didn't acknowledge both his sources of inspiration as well as final execution.

My deepest personal gratitude goes to those distinguished scholars at the University of California, Davis. Specifically, to Drs. Albert J. Winkler and Maynard A. Amerine, my revered teachers and close friends. No one can write about grapes without consulting Dr. H. P. Olmo, one of the world's leading viticulturists and geneticists. Nor for that matter without turning to Harold W. Berg, Emeritus Professor and former Chairman of the Department of Viticulture and Enology at Davis. A. N. Kasimatis, Extension Viticulturist at U.C. Davis, was also an invaluable guide. No one, I believe, has ever been so fortunate to claim such an illustrious group of purists as inspirational figures.

However, any weaknesses or shortcomings of this book rest squarely with the author, not with his mentors. But I am grateful to those who offered considerable assistance in outlining and in editing the text. Personal thanks are extended to Paul Moser, Ralph Rundell, and Norman Roby, and most especially to the great calligrapher and constant friendly advisor, Arthur L. Davies, without whose artistic advice and encouragement this ampelography would not exist.

Contents

White Wine Varieties

Red Wine Varieties

Biographical Sketches

Glossary

For Doris

Chardonnay

plate 1

Chardonnay

Viticultural Profile:

The Chardonnay is a vigorous growing vine, but is only moderately productive. In California's cool coastal valleys, it will bear four to five tons per acre, when cane—or long-pruned. Normally, for maximum quality, the yield is lower.

Its vigorous shoots grow semi-upright with large entire to moderately three-lobed leaves. The glabrous leaves are glossy-green when young and dull, dark green and somewhat roughened when mature. Most of the mature leaves have the primary veins exposed, or naked, at the petiolar sinus, making this variety easily distinguished from other small-clustered white varieties.

The cluster is small, cylindrical and usually winged. It can be well-filled to compact, with small round, thin-skinned berries that develop a deep yellow-green to amber color when ripe. The mature fruit has a distinctive rich, fruity flavor, though it has no discernible aroma.

Chardonnay is an early-ripener. In California it can be subjected to excessively high mid-summer temperatures as it matures. Its early maturity and thin-skinned, soft-pulped berries make the Chardonnay an easy target for birds. As a result, serious crop loss can occur in vineyards near wooded areas. Chardonnay is recommended for cultivation only in the cooler wine regions of California.

To say that the Chardonnay produces superb dry white wines is a little like saying Michelangelo was a great artist. True indeed, but something of a grave injustice at the same time. Just as the particular artistic creations of this great artist are more important than the original generality, so it is much more valuable to know the Chardonnay through its rich and rewarding diversity.

And what a diversity.

The Chardonnay variety is not just Champagne, nor Pouilly-Fuissé, not simply Montrachet, Meursault, Chablis, nor the "Chardonnay" of America. It is all of these and more. In Chardonnay's homeland of France alone, its versatility is astonishing.

In the officially delimited region of France known as Champagne, around the picturesque village of Épernay and south of the magnificent cathedral town of Reims, the Chardonnay lends its delicacy and perfumed subtleties to the solidity and depth of the Pinot noir and Pinot Meunier to produce the original sparkling magic which has been imitated the world over. Some Champagne houses blend in the best years a particular cuvée, called "Blanc de Blancs," which is a 100% solo performance by the Chardonnay, spotlighting all of its regal, clean flavor and delightful freshness.

Another interpretation of the Chardonnay is rendered in the tiny region known as Chablis, just east of Auxerre 120 kilometers southwest of the Champagne district. Here the Chardonnay is generally called the Beaunois, though other current aliases include Aubaine, Arnoison and Melon blanc. In this famous district it produces wines of seven Grand Cru vineyards, twenty-two excellent Premier Crus, as well as those of the less prestigious areas entitled only to the appellations "Chablis" or "Petit Chablis."

Without question it would take the administrative skills of a Hammurabi, the diplomacy of a Dag Hammarskjold, and the nerve of Napoleon to iron out all the misrepresentations involving "Chablis". Genuine Chablis has a bright, greenish-yellow color, a crisp and refined aroma, (made only from the Chardonnay) a delicate fruity flavor with a cutting-edge firmness hovering in the background.

The description should serve as some explanation for the wine's popularity and for the consequent widespread sale of bogus "Chablis" before the passage of France's controlled appellation laws in 1936. It also explains the use of the name Chablis in many countries of the world, including the U.S., to describe generic wines (wines carrying regional names) which have nothing to do with genuine Chablis. No one would argue that "generics" don't serve a great need and can be of high quality. But there is no doubt that use of the name outside of Chablis is insufficiently specific and may be potentially misleading.

The Chardonnay's personality changes again as we move south and slightly east from the Champagne and Chablis districts. From a delicate, rather pale northerner, it becomes a warm, jovial companion with an air of subtlety and opulence which the variety shares with its famous motherland, the Côte d'Or (the 'slope of gold') of northern Burgundy.

These are wines the French describe as "_charnu_"—fleshy, or ripe. With exceptions, the finest among them come from the southerly townships of the Côte: Meursault, Puligny-Montrachet and Chassagne-Montrachet. Those of the former are softer, drier, often more elegant than those of the latter two, which are luscious golden affairs which resolve layer upon layer into a multi-faceted and unforgettable flavor impression. In great years, the men who make masterpieces such as Le Montrachet or Chevalier-Montrachet rightfully consider them beyond criticism. The wines are simply themselves, incomparable.

Other small but superb plantings of Chardonnay are to be found further north on the Côte, at Corton-Charlemagne, at the Clos Blanc de Vougeot and at Musigny—wines of exquisite beauty. Many Burgundians firmly believe that some of the red wines of Musigny owe their finesse and elegance in part to skillful blending with the Chardonnay, since 15% of the vines planted may legally be Chardonnay or Pinot blanc, the white-fruited form of the Pinot noir.

It is well to mention in passing that until recently these two varieties (Charonnay and Pinot blanc) were thought to be identical. It is only now that the word "_Pinot_" which has traditionally been linked to "Chardonnay" is beginning to disappear from the wine labels in recognition of the Chardonnay's viticultural individuality and unique quality. "Pinot Chardonnay" is a definite misnomer.

Farther south in Burgundy, the much vaster growing regions of the Châlonnais, the Mâconnais and the Beaujolais also owe the quality of their wine at least partially to the Chardonnay. In Beaujolais Blanc it is frequently blended with much larger quantities of the lesser Aligoté, while in the wines of the Chalonnais and Mâconnais, it is paired with the Pinot blanc. Among this wide array of wines, best known would certainly be the straightforward and lively Pouilly-Fuissé, a Mâconnais often more generous than Chablis, but with some of the same mineral-like goût de terroir (taste of the soil). Pouilly-Fuissé is limited by variety to the Chardonnay, and geographically to the five communes of Solutré, Fuissé, Pouilly, Chaintré and Vergisson. Closely related though not so well known are the Chardonnays from the nearby communes of Pouilly-Loché, Pouilly-Vinzelles, and the St. Véran District.

Negligible amounts of Chardonnay are also found in other areas of France, such as Alsace and the Loire Valley, where it lends its acidity and balance to various blends.

But the rest of the really shiny stars in Chardonnay's galaxy come not from France, but from California wineries. Depending on where your loyalties lie it may be surprising, gratifying, or even embarrassing, but the fact remains; it is difficult if not impossible to distinguish California's finest Chardonnays from the better offerings of the French Côte d'Or. There is no exaggeration in naming it

California's finest white, if not finest wine. Especially in the cooler pockets of the coastal counties the variety shows a remarkable sugar/acid balance, and when traditionally vinified, equally remarkable aging capacity. Small amounts of most pleasing carefully vinifed Chardonnay are made in the Finger Lakes district and on the Niagara peninsula by skilled winemakers. To date, climate and man have not yet given those eastern relatives the depth of the amazing Chardonnays of California and Europe.

The variety's congenital liabilities are not easily overlooked. It tends to be a shy-bearer and much more discouraging, is very susceptible to a whole roster of maladies. Particularly troublesome are the problems of soil-borne viruses, mildews and poor flowering (coulure) which produces small, unseeded "shot" berries (millerandage.)

These difficulties have given the Chardonnay something of a tarnished image in many countries, and have put off all but the most dedicated growers. Happily, the viticulturists at the University of California at Davis have provided healthy strains of the plant, and on that basis it is reasonable to expect an expansion of the relatively small acreages in countries such as Rumania, Chile, Australia, South Africa, and the Soviet Union.

In Argentina it is well represented, though usually blended too heavily with the White Riesling and the Italian Riesling.

The only other notable producer of an unblended wine is Australia, which makes a clean, thoroughly sound table wine from Chardonnay, there often called "White Pinot".

The newest plantings are in Bulgaria and New Zealand, both of which are enjoying some success.

In writing of Chardonnay's overall reputation, one feels obligated to trot out expressions of highest praise. And rightly so. Granted that superlatives have slithered very handily onto paper in this case, but their use seems easily defensible. They aren't likely to find truer application than to the Chardonnay.

Pinot Blanc

plate 2

Pinot Blanc

Viticultural Profile:

Pinot blanc is at best moderately vigorous; its yield, too, is moderate. The vine ideally should carry only a fair-sized crop, and growers must carefully prune in order to reduce potential crop size. Most often, it is short or spur-pruned.

In growth habit, the vine is quite upright. Its deep green colored leaves are large, full, and rough. Clusters are small to small-medium in size, and long-conical to cylindrical in shape. Often they are winged. Flower set is quite good, and the clusters are often compact, which makes them vulnerable to late rains, with a tendency toward bunch rot under damp conditions.

The berries are pale-yellow in color, at times with a yellow-green tint. They are small, round, and when mature, have a neutral vinous flavor.

As a moderate producer whose wines depend on the quality of the fruit, Pinot blanc is better adapted to the cooler wine growing regions of the world. In California, it is recommended for the north coastal counties. One disadvantage of Pinot blanc is that the skin of the berry has a high tannin content, unusual for a white wine variety. This natural tannin carries over inevitably into both the 'must' (unfermented juice) and the wines. In warmer growing regions, the 'musts' tend to be too low in total acidity.

In all regions, there is a tendency toward darkening so special care by the winemaker must be taken to prevent this.

Many of the older Pinot blanc vineyards in California have been infected with the undesirable leafroll virus, which has contributed to its status as only a qualified recommended variety for California vineyards. The successful efforts to develop virus-free clones at the University of California, have led to renewed interest in Pinot blanc.

Pinot blanc is a distinguished member of the prestigious Pinot family of wine grapes, or rather one should say this is so of the "true" Pinot blanc. The grape's identity has been obscured by numerous local synonyms and by its frequent confusion with the Chardonnay. In European vineyards the plantings are often mixed; particularly in the Côte d'Or of Burgundy and in other famous regions of France. Sometimes the vineyards consist of mixed plantings of Pinot blanc and Chardonnay. This historical precedent has led to a confusion in the Chablis District, where the local name for Chardonnay is none other than "Pinot blanc".

In recent years, viticulturists have concluded that Chardonnay, which is often erroneously called Pinot Chardonnay, is not a member of the Pinot clan. It is a distinct variety which technically should be called simply Chardonnay, when referring to both the grape and the wine. This mistaken Pinot identity abounds throughout the wine world. But the fact is that there are distinct morphological differences setting them clearly apart; Pinot blanc when compared with Chardonnay demonstrates different growth habits, leaf shape and texture, and seed morphology. In the vineyards, the two ripen at different times, yield musts with different qualities, and produce wines that are certainly different in flavor. Though they are often called cousins, there actually is no close relation between Pinot blanc and Chardonnay.

Pinot blanc is most likely derived from the Pinot noir (a red variety) through genetic accident. A color change of the fruit, through mutation, is not uncommon with wine grapes.

Its history is much briefer, yet more entangled than that of Pinot noir. In fact, Pinot blanc was for centuries not distinguished from Chardonnay. It attracted little if any attention until after the Congress of Chalons when the French began to recognize its individuality. Its origins are clouded, though several sources have traced it back to the 16th century. By the 17th century, it was firmly entrenched in Burgundy vineyards, and had made its way to other European wine regions, even to Russia. Today, we find it cultivated in almost every wine country, often, alas, having acquired a local variant name through time.

In California where quality-seeking wine producers adopted the varietal nomenclature after Prohibition, Pinot blanc was one of the first varietal wines to appear. California was in fact probably the first region to print Pinot blanc on a wine label.

Yet, simplicity has not reigned in the New World either. Here, Pinot blanc has frequently been confused with the Chenin blanc, as one of the misnomers for the latter wine is "White Pinot," a name that happily is disappearing. Chenin blanc, also called Pineau de la Loire, (a classic French Loire Valley variety) is another white wine grape that is distinct and unrelated to the Pinot blanc.

But now in spite of the fact that the Pinot blanc has been successfully identified as a distinct wine grape, its plantings have not increased in the California vineyards in proportion to the recent explosion involving other celebrated wine grapes. One possible explanation may be that in the various French Burgundy regions its use in many of the wines is decreasing primarily due to its runner-up status compared to the Chardonnay. In the Burgundian Côte d'Or, however, the old confusion still exists, and many of the famous vineyards remain mixed. It is probable that prestigious wines such as Puligny-Montrachet and Chassagne-Montrachet are made from a good percentage of Pinot blanc in concert with Chardonnay. Some of the lesser wines such as Beaujolais Blanc, now mostly grown in the northern plots, near the city of Mâcon, can be made from either of these two grapes, or blends of the two.

French growers and producers are not oriented toward varietal thinking; —i.e., putting the grape variety on the label. They are, instead, directed toward their growth and production laws of Appellation Contrôlée, with either estate or regional labeling. In Burgundy, the regulations apply to certain permissable grape varieties and to rigorous controls in the vineyard and in the cellar.

The permitted great white variety is the Chardonnay which as discussed above may, in some French plantings be Pinot blanc. Chardonnay yields no more than about 2 tons per acre in Burgundy's Côte d'Or. In the other communes, maximum yield is around 2 1/2 tons per acre. In fact when the production comes up to 3 or 3 1/2 tons per acre the difference is noted and the wine is allowed a lesser appellation. With an excess crop, considered to be anything over 3 1/2 tons per acre, the wine is subsequently declassified as "Bourgogne Blanc," without any approved appellation contrôlée for a commune or cru. The fact is however, the generic Bourgogne Blanc wines can be quite good wines when made in a good to excellent vintage.

In California where the economics of winegrowing are different and in some ways more demanding, grapes which yield three or four tons per acre are considered to be meager producers, difficult to grow on a commercial scale. Perhaps, what with the general lack of recognition for Pinot blanc as a grape, and with the necessity to secure an economically feasible yield per acre, California Pinot blanc wines have not been grown and allowed to show their best features. It is an established fact in viticulture, whenever wines are forced to carry an excessively large crop, there is always a corresponding loss of quality and character. It just may be that for this reason, Pinot blanc has been unable to make the transition from the Old World to the New.

When all is considered, the Pinot blanc seems deserving of greater attention. This variety, when grown in cool climates and carefully fermented, offers a high quality wine of distinct aroma and flavor. Also, the grapes develop adequate sugar content and natural acidity, producing wines with balance and smoothness. The 'must' does have a tendency to darken; however, with the widespread us of temperature-controlled stainless steel fermentors, and the increasing interest in field crushing grapes in the vineyards, this tendency could be averted.

But what has delayed Pinot blanc's progress in California where there is no confusion between it and Chardonnay is the fact that only recently the experts at U.C. Davis have been so successful in isolating virus-free clonal selections for Chardonnay. These are more productive, without loss of wine quality, and are highly adaptable to the cooler districts of the state. This may explain why Pinot blanc, which has only recently been available virus-free, has been lost in the wine grape explosion.

In other regions of the world lacking the superior clones of Chardonnay, Pinot blanc is rather ubiquitous. The Alsatians are quite proud of their Pinot blanc. In this picturesque northeastern part of France, the white wines are drier and fuller-bodied than those of their German neighbors. Alsatian Pinot blanc offers a delicacy, a crisp acidity, and pleasant body to accompany the superb local cuisine. It is one of the few varieties designated as the finest of Alsace according to a decree in 1962.

Across the border, Pinot blanc is known in Germany as either Weissburgunder or as Klevner, and is not widely planted. The grape goes by the Weissburgunder, Klevner, or Clevner Blanc names in Austria, with most of the wines labeled as 'Weisser Burgunder.' The Swiss love their wines to be youthful and with some acidity; consequently, there is a good percentage of Pinot blanc cultivated. But in Northeastern Italy in the Trentino-Alto-Adige district, the grape has acquired several different names in this viticulturally mixed district. Austrians call it Weissburgunder, and Italians refer to it as Pinot Bianco or as Borgogna Bianco, where it is widely cultivated, being used for either everyday white wine or as a base for sparkling wines. The Alto-Adige wine district has made remarkable advances in the production of quality sparkling wines, a few of which are made by the traditional champagne method. In the Piedmont District (northeastern Italy) near the village of Alba, a very agreeable white wine is made from Pinot blanc (sold as "Pinot d'Alba") and packaged in a tall, slender green bottle. A small acreage of Pinot blanc is cultivated in Lombardy, east of Piedmont.

Pinot blanc is said to have been introduced into Chile around 1850. Today it is thriving in both Uruguay and Argentina where it is considered to share top honors for white wines with the Sémillon. There are also scattered plantings in Japan, the Soviet Union, and Luxembourg. In recent plantings in the Pacific Northwest region of the United States, Pinot blanc has passed the experimental stages in both the Yakima Valley of Washington State and in parts of Oregon. In these cool growing areas, the variety develops a nice balance and taste, with an agreeable high acidity, and may prove exciting in the near future.

Of all the white burgundy-type wine grapes, Pinot blanc runs a creditable second to Chardonnay. In that competition, to place second is no disgrace. Its future in France seems likely to remain important because of the mixed plantings. In California it is increasing in favor with the producers of white wines who appreciate its quality and high acidity. In the foreseeable future, it may be joined with Chenin blanc or another similar grape to improve the quality of white generic wines or to be ideally produced under its own "varietal" banner.

Since there will always be dedicated winemakers looking for very special wines to make, Pinot blanc should remain with us as one of the great grapes for many years.

White Riesling

plate 3

White Riesling

Viticultural Profile:

The White Riesling is both moderately vigorous and productive. With long or cane-pruning it is capable of bearing five to six tons per acre on good sites in California's coastal valleys. Higher quality results are obtained at 3-4 tons per acre.

The semi-upright shoots provide good shade coverage for the fruit. The leaves are medium-sized, round, and usually three-lobed. They are dull-green above with noticeable tomentum below. The shoot tips, petioles (see glossary) and tendrils are characterized by a purple-red pigmentation in late season.

The clusters are small, winged, and quite compact at maturity. The berries are small, round, greenish-yellow in color and often have a speckled appearance due to the small dot-like lenticels on the skin. The berry is tender-skinned and soft when ripe. White Riesling is known to be a late-season ripener. Bunch rot can be a serious problem in the event of late rains.

The true Riesling, Germany's magnificent gift to the world's great white wines, is technically the "White Riesling" in order to distinguish it from its shirttail relatives. Three of these, the "Grey Riesling", "Walschriesling" (Italian Riesling) and the "Missouri

Riesling", actually have no true Riesling ancestry. However, the Sylvaner (Franken Riesling), Emerald Riesling (a University of California cross of White Riesling and Muscadelle du Bordelais), and the Müller-Thurgau (a Riesling x Sylvaner cross) can all lay small claim to the bloodline as cousins.

Under ideal conditions, the noble White Riesling can yield a wine which may possibly be the pinnacle of the white wine world, or at least a serious challenger for that honor with the greatest Chardonnays. An exquisite flavor, a caressing soft texture, an opulence of bouquet, and an attractive variance in sweetness combine to make the White Riesling a source of immense pleasure to the casual wine drinker and an object of adoration and gustatory complexity to the experienced wine buff.

Many ampelographers believe the White Riesling is indigenous to the banks of the Rhine, while a few suspect it may be the variety called 'Argitis', once cultivated by the Romans along the Rhone River in the 3rd Century. The grape's recorded history dates from the first extensive plantings on slopes along the Rhine River in the early 12th Century. But it wasn't until 1716 with the codification of German viticultural practices that the vine's premium qualities received official recognition. Lesser varieties were uprooted and replaced by the Riesling, as growers soon came to prefer its obvious intrinsic qualities over more productive, hardier, and less distinguished varieties.

Today, possibly even more than in that epoch, the Riesling towers over its German vinous colleagues: the Sylvaner, the Müller-Thurgau, the Traminer, the Ruländer (the French Pinot gris), the Klevner (French Pinot blanc), and many others. As outstanding as it is alongside its brethren, there has evolved a quality hierarchy within the family of White Riesling wines. It is explained by the story of the absentminded bishop whose permission was necessary to begin the harvest. In 1775 it seems that he simply forgot to order picking to begin in the vineyards around Hochheim. Some accounts exonerate him, claiming his messengers were beset upon by bandits. The local growers experienced great anxiety about their moldy and apparently ruined crop. Eventually, wines were made from the sorry-looking, shriveled grapes harvested so late. But the grapes were infected by a beneficial mold, and the wines set the precedent for what we now know as Edelfäule (noble rot) wines.

The legal classification which evolved over centuries from this miracle-by-negligence helped divide German wines into levels of sweetness and flavor intensity. The classification is now based on the weight of the must (unfermented juice) which is basically the degree of sugar concentration. Usually, the sugar concentration receives a boost from the benign mold (scientifically _Botrytis cinerea_) which affects the mature grapes. When Nature cooperates by bringing warm, wet weather for a full day followed by a period of low humidity, mycelia of this mold pierce the soft-skinned berries, permitting evaporation and concentrating the sugar content.

The special wines range from _Spätlese_ (late-picked, riper, slightly sweeter than standard table wines) to _Auslese_ quality (made from specially selected bunches of overripe grape and thus sweeter yet). Then, when the botrytis mold has developed, one moves on to the inner circle of this oligarchy: the _Beerenauslese_ and _Trockenbeerenauslese_ levels. Both of these rare wines comparable to golden nectar are made by a painstaking, berry-by-berry selection of botrytised grapes. They are extraordinary rich, sweet, wines capable of a remarkable lifespan and worthy of the high prices they fetch.

Unfortunately, even in its preferred environment the noble Riesling can be a great headache, occasionally leading to a migraine. Yet without question, its optimum quality is obtained in its native Germany where it is planted in the most northerly location possible for the _vinifera_ (Old World) varieties. On the steep slopes of the Rhine and Moselle Rivers it makes the most out of the sun exposure and microclimate, growing in schist and granitic soils which hold the sun's heat. While apparently enjoying a little stress and struggle, the Riesling remains fundamentally temperamental—demanding, relcacitrant, and fragile. Its soft-skinned berries arranged in compact clusters are easy targets for various rots, unbeneficial molds, and ever-threatening frosts. Each year, all the artistic talent and determination of the winemaker are drawn upon to realize the grape's full potential.

The Riesling is grown, with varying degrees of success, in many other countries. There are fine plantings in France's Alsace, in Austria, Switzerland, Northern Italy, Yugoslavia, South Africa, the Soviet Union, Australia, Chile, and of course, in California. Occasionally, the California wines are labeled "White

Riesling" but, more often, "Johannisberg Riesling." On United States wine labels, the name "Riesling" is no guarantee that White Riesling is in the bottle. "Riesling" by itself may mean that the wine was made from Sylvaner, the Grey Riesling (not a Riesling at all, but the French Chauché gris), the Emerald Riesling, or the Missouri Riesling, a North American hybrid whose wines don't resemble White Riesling at all.

However, there are small pockets of California vineyards where this variety yields wines bearing a genuine resemblance to those made in Germany and neighboring Alsace. Subtle, delicate White Rieslings have been made from small valleys north of Santa Cruz and the cooler hillsides of Napa and Sonoma Counties. Promising new regions in California are beginning to produce fine Rieslings in some quantity; the signs have been encouraging from the Salinas Valley of Monterey County, parts of Santa Barbara County, and in selected locations in eastern Washington State and western Oregon. New York State winemakers have also attracted attention with their remarkably fine Rieslings. The primary problem for them is vine survival in the extremely cold winters.

There are, thankfully, many dedicated growers of Riesling in many wine-producing nations. Challenged by this noble grape, they steadfastly hold to the belief that their quest for those perfect combinations of slope, sun exposure, soil and moisture will yield great and highly individualized wines. In a sense, then, though the eminence of German White Riesling is solidly established, the world-wide story is far from over.

Sylvaner

plate 4

Sylvaner

<u>Viticultural Profile</u>:

A vine of medium vigor and medium-high productivity, the Sylvaner buds late and ripens early; in California it thrives best with spur-pruning.

Its leaf is nearly round. The superior sinuses (see glossary) fold over one another and the petiolar sinus is deep but narrow, adding to the round impression. It is yellow-green in color—practically without hairs on either surface.

Clusters are small to medium in size. They are cylindrical in shape and very compact, to the point of distorting the shapes of the berries, which are medium, spherical, pulpy, and dotted with lenticels when ripe. Their skins are dark yellow-green to amber-yellow (the latter caused by more exposure to the sun).

A good characterization of the Sylvaner variety might be a "thick-skinned old cuss from Austria." This unassuming and enthusiastic fellow has made quite a few friends down through the years; partly no doubt because of his vigor, rugged constitution and consistent performance.

When a grower finds a variety that is relatively disease-resistant, late budding, early ripening and almost insanely fertile, he is likely to find room for it no matter what he has already planted. And this has meant the great success of the Sylvaner, possessor of all these qualities and more. It can shrug off a late spring frost and go on to a normal output because of its enormous number of fertile buds, and will regularly produce pleasant wine even when planted in less favored locations, as it often is in Germany.

If it can be said to have any performance problem at all, it is in fermentation: The "meat" of the Sylvaner is very thick and pulpy, and will not easily give a good clean 'must' (unfermented juice) unless carefully and expertly treated by the wine-maker.

Unfortunately, the overall enthusiasm generated by the vine itself does not extend to most of the wines. The usual Sylvaner is best drunk young, and without the formality of lengthy barrel or bottle aging. It can be very dry and tart, as the Alsatians make it, or softly sweet, as in eastern Europe, but in both cases its chief virtues are lightness and freshness. Rarely does it have much in the way of superb finish or real flair.

There are very noteworthy exceptions. All of these come from Germany (where Sylvaner is the most planted variety); more specifically from Franconia, around the town of Würzburg, seventy miles east of the Rheinhessen. Here the Franken Riesling, as it is called, produces wines with more style and assertiveness than one would expect from a Sylvaner. Especially when late-picked, they take on a peculiarly attractive and highly prized _bodenton_, an elusive suggestion of mineral flavors the best examples of which are found in the "Stein" wines of Würzburg, along with those of Ipfhofen and Eschendorf.

In other German regions, i.e., the Nahe, Baden, the Rheingau, Rheinhessen and Palatinate, the vine is also known as the _Oestereicher_ and shares space with favored German varieties such as the White Riesling, Traminer and the Müller-Thurgau. Its greatest strongholds are the Rheinhessen and the southern Palatinate (the Oberhaardt), where it constitutes upwards of 75 percent of some communal areas. This contrasts sharply with the situation in the Rheingau, for example, where only 15 percent of the total acreage is Sylvaner.

The wines of Germany's neighbors in Europe vary widely in style, but none approaches the quality of the Franken wines. It can be a challenge even to identify the variety and its wines in many of these countries because of an impressive, if confusing, list of aliases.

In France's Alsace and Lorraine, and on the east bank of the Luxembourgeoise Moselle, it is the _Feuille Ronde_, _Clozier_, _Frankentraube_ or _Gentil Vert_, while Swiss growers on the east end of Lake Geneva know it as the _Plant du Rhin_, _Gros Rhin_, or _Gros Riesling_. A very prominent vine in Hungary, it is found under the labels _Sylvani Zold_, _Pepltraube_, _Cilifanti_ and _Zirfandler_, the latter being a spelling variation on its Austrian name, _Zierfandler_. Italy's Trentino-Alto Aldige produces a small amount of Zierfandler for a rather common dry wine. The south central and eastern sections of Czechoslovakia and the Drava River basin of Yugoslavia make from it a markedly sweeter wine which is quite good.

In America, the Sylvaner is not an overwhelming presence. Even after the big rush to plant this variety in the first few years of this decade, it amounted to only about 1,675 acres in California. This is curious in a sense, because in cooler areas it produces as pleasant and balanced a wine, relatively speaking, as the White Riesling; but it has been effectively eclipsed by its more aristocratic comrade. Our varietal-conscious market probably accounts for this phenomenon.

And it is true that the Sylvaner's inland valley, warm climate cultivation has been very disappointing. The wines are coarse and lifeless almost to the point of being unpalatable. The better wines which are being made, those from Napa and Sonoma for example, are unfortunately often labeled "Riesling", and should not be confused with the White (or Johannisberg) Riesling.

A surprisingly productive refuge of the Sylvaner is the Yakima Valley of Washington State. Only since the repeal of Prohibition have examples of _Vitis_ _vinifera_ been producing in any quantity there, but Sylvaner very early on proved its ability to flourish in that climate.

Emerald Riesling

plate 5

Emerald Riesling

Viticultural Profile:

A vigorous, productive grape variety, Emerald Riesling can quite comfortably produce from 8 to 12 tons per acre on good soils. Quite fruitful when spur-pruned, its normal growth habit is semi-upright to trailing, with long sturdy canes. Hybridized at the University of California at Davis in 1935, it was selected for commercial cultivation because of its high quality fruit and its adaptability to a wide range of soils and climates, including warm regions in California's interior valley.

Emerald Riesling ripens during the early mid-season and, even in the warmer climates yields an excellent crop with fine natural acidity. At maturity, the leaves are large and round with practically no lobes (see glossary); both the upper and lower surfaces are smooth and glabrous.

Large and conical in shape, the clusters vary from loose to well-filled, with the individual berry being medium-sized, round, and firmly attached to the pedicel. At maturity the berries develop a distinctive and easily recognized deep bluish-green color. The soft pulp of the berry is gelatinous in texture, but fortunately, the thick, tough skin protects the mature berry from rotting.

As its name implies, Emerald Riesling is one of those colorful varieties people seldom forget. First of all, its must (unfermented juice) has an undesirable tendency toward browning which means that rapid harvesting and immediate crushing are imperative. Also, the pulpy, gelatinous nature of the must requires prompt separation of the free-run juice—another essential for quality. But even after these skillful manipulations are completed, Emerald Riesling "musts" tend to be murky in color which, along with the high natural acidity, makes fermentation a slow and potentially difficult procedure. Winemakers, knowing they have a problem on their hands, call upon assistance from technology; often, wineries will use efficient centrifuges to remove the soluble solids before fermenting in temperature-controlled stainless steel fermentors. These expensive clarification devices are nowadays practically universal in the California wine country.

Having conquered the temperamental problems, the vintners are later rewarded to see the fermented wine fall brilliantly clear and, also, become extremely stable. For aesthetic compensation, the wine retains a most attractive pale-green hue which comes from the charming light-green color of the free-run juice. Thus, the reason behind the name of Emerald Riesling is obvious.

Technically, Emerald Riesling is an intraspecific cross. This is so because both of its parents—White Riesling and the Muscadelle—are members of the same species of grapes, the prestigious _Vitis vinifera_. On the other hand, a species "hybrid" grape results from cross-breeding members of two different species, i.e., _vinifera_ with _labrusca_. The beauty of both a hybrid and a cross is that often they incorporate the best of two worlds. Emerald Riesling does so nicely by combining the productivity and adaptability of its slightly muscat-flavored Muscadelle parent along with the acidity and delicate aromatic qualities of the noble German Riesling.

Sometimes random chance provides the impetus, as was indeed the case with Emerald Riesling, but quite frequently today the wealth of genetic science is applied to plant breeding to bring us better and unique wine grapes. The world's leading institution in the science of plant breeding is the University of California at Davis.

It was back in 1933 that Dr. Olmo, the University's distinguished geneticist, began his lifelong project: the breeding of new grape varieties specifically adapted to the unique conditions of California viticulture. You may well wonder why such a program was started since almost all of the European _vinifera_ grapes have been successfully transplanted to California and their wines can compete today with Europe's finest. But the underlying philosophy is basically that through plant breeding one can develop wine grapes especially for the many unique climates of California. Wines produced from grapes bred in and for California can result in tastes that are pleasingly unique and perhaps more in tune with American palates.

Explaining the philosophy is much easier for us than controlling the many variables involved in genetics for the skilled geneticists. Suffice it to say that vine breeding is an intricate and elaborate procedure, requiring anywhere between fifteen to 25 years from start to finish. Years pass while the vine is tested for production and adaptability, and more years go by while the wines are analyzed by experts. Plant breeding, a lifelong task, requires determination, technical genius, a great deal of pluck and even a little luck. Luck assisted the emergence of Emerald Riesling, and the result was close to perfect.

To explain, in the early experimental vineyards on the Davis campus, there were several Muscadelle vines planted close to a row of Riesling vines. In 1935 a few of the Muscadelle berries had become accidentally pollen contaminated by the adjacent White Riesling. From this fortuitous fluke cross-pollination, the alert researchers collected and planted the rare seeds. By 1939, the first trial wines were made from the 22 vines under cultivation. For comparative purposes, the trial was repeated the following years from 10 vines planted in the cooler Napa Valley.

To everyone's pleasant surprise, the vines were distinguished by their productivity, adaptability, and healthy foliage, and the wines offered fine sensory features to match. They displayed a clean and fresh aroma with a trace of Muscat, and the flavors were fruity and tart. Clearly, even by the high standards of the Davis experts, the wine stood in the well-above-average category. Follow-up tests ensued as a natural precautionary measure, checking for resistance to diseases and making sure the vine was virus-free.

It wasn't until 1946 that Emerald Riesling made its illustrious debut on an experimental basis in commercial vineyards. The Paul Masson Winery was one of the first to cultivate and later sell this bright new star commercially. Emerald Riesling, first considered to be a blending wine, immediately exceeded this modest expectation. In a now historic wine tasting that took place at the Palace Hotel in San Francisco in 1955, the first commercial bottlings carrying the varietal name were sampled by a large panel of experts. One can well imagine the shocked expressions of those who later learned the name of the wine that pleased them and had earned their high praises.

Yet more time was required before Emerald Riesling was accepted in California. From hindsight, we can well understand this, since it was one of the very first totally new wine grapes in the world. By 1965 only 400 acres were planted in all of California, but the small quantity of wine produced served as its best public relations, presenting a convincing argument to any doubters. Today there are almost 3,000 acres planted, and Emerald Riesling has become a popular standard varietal wine, truly unique to America.

Yet it still retained its unique personality, as winegrowers located in cooler climates learned to their chagrin. This fine wine variety was better suited to warmer regions; thus, it is favored by growers in the vast Central Valley and a few other warm vineyard lands. The timing of this realization was a real boon to wine consumers, coming right before the wine boom in America.

Emerald Riesling, along with several other warm climate varieties, enabled producers to supply clean, sprightly table wines offering character and economy, an unbeatable combination. America's answer to "vin de table" were called by some "Valley Varietals."

Emerald Riesling has indeed broadened the taste spectrum by filling a real need and fulfilling the goals of the University grape breeding programs. Other unique crosses have since been introduced into commercial vineyards, and soon we have other delightful new wines with such enchanting names as Carnelian, Centurion, and Carmine. Accolades will doubtless fall their way, and these new, original wines will have an easier time being accepted by wine lovers. Emerald Riesling, that fortuitous accident of nature, has paved the way for them.

Grey Riesling

plate 6

Grey Riesling

Viticultural Profile:

    This variety is a strong, vigorous producer capable of yielding five to seven tons per acre. It ripens in late August in California's Central Valley, later in the coastal counties. Harvest timing should be exact. The canes are semi-erect; spur pruning is standard practice.

    The leaves are small, rough, and only slightly lobed. The berries are medium-sized, long-oval, dull reddish-tan in color and somewhat firm. The clusters are small-medium in size, conical and shouldered. Their compactness creates some risk of bunch rot.

    During the 1940's and '50's, the decades in which table wine was a vast and rather alien subject for all but a handful of Americans, the "Grey Riesling" experienced something of a golden era. It was the bottle of white wine which frequently appeared on banquet and Thanksgiving Day tables, or even when company came to call, satisfying the thirst for wine and wine knowledge of an only casually interested public.

    The complication of the plot came with the "wine boom" of the 1960's. Paying more careful attention to the growing number of wine authorities, the budding wine buffs made some disturbing discoveries about the finer varieties and the wines they produce. A few jaws had to drop at the realization that the Grey Riesling is not any sort of Riesling at all, (that is, not related or similar to the true White Riesling of Germany) but rather the _Chauché Gris_, a French variety found commonly in the _departements_ of Vienne and Charente. Adding to this the rather low esteem in which the French hold it, and the fact that it is permitted in no controlled appellation wines in that entire country, and we had a full-scale expose on our hands. There began something of a reaction against this old favorite, during which many Americans forsook it in favor of Sauvignon blanc, Chardonnay, the White Riesling and other more exalted members of the _Vitis vinifera_ (Old World) clan.

But the dénouement of the story, in the late sixties and seventies, brought the Grey Riesling full circle. As prices for the finest wines soared, and the initial, self-conscious snobbery of some wine enthusiasts began to subside, people rediscovered the Grey Riesling for what it was: a simple clean note in wine's music—a rather dry white wine graced with a pleasing, grapy flavor, and healthy acidities.

Its low-profile character made it versatile and its modest price made it accessible. No one was asking for more. It surpassed its old popularity and currently enjoys a position of eminence among California's collection of honest and pleasing "drinking wines".

California's introduction to this vine, this Chauché Gris, took place sometime in the mid-nineteenth century. Judging from the lack of detailed information, no one considered it a momentous event. The variety has since been known as Gray Duchess and more often as Grey Riesling, but something about that latter name caught America's fancy soon after the repeal of Prohibition, when it was offered as such by the Wente Brothers of Livermore Valley. Today, more than thirty wineries produce a "varietal" bottling under that label.

Extensive vineyard experiments have revealed it as a rather accommodating fellow, producing very passable wines in all but the coolest and warmest of California's wine districts. Its greatest concentrations are found in Napa, Monterey and Alameda counties: the former producing fainter, less full and perhaps less satisfying wines, while the latter two yield rounder, deeper results. The variety's favorite haunt is the Livermore Valley, east of the San Francisco Bay. The wines from these gravelly soils maintain the greatest consistency in terms of ripe flavors and the absence of coarseness.

Thought not too particular about where it is planted, the "Grey Riesling" can get a little persnickety around harvest time. Because it ripens early and has a relatively short peak maturity period, it must be watched closely. More than with other varieties of its caliber, careful timing is required in picking and crushing to obtain the optimum sugar-acid balance.

Müller-Thurgau

plate 7

Müller-Thurgau

<u>*Viticultural Profile:*</u>

This variety is vigorous and productive, with semi-upright canes. It has bright-green to yellow-green foliage. The leaves are large, deeply five-lobed. The cluster is medium-large, winged and conical to irregular in shape.

The berry is long-oval with a green tint of color.

The strong vine is productive and quite fruitful with short- or spur-pruning. It should produce six to eight tons per acre in good soils and cool climates.

A description of wine made from the little-known Müller-Thurgau variety is not likely to include poetic rapture. There might be an occasional superlative or exclamation point, but in general its story is told with moderate enthusiasm. No medieval traditions here, no romance, no great authors or kings publicly praising this "noble wine". But the Müller-Thurgau story does have honesty and hard work behind it, as well as great promise ahead of it—for those taking the time to look.

In order to produce the vine which today carries his name, Dr. Müller-Thurgau (Thurgau was the maiden name of his wife), a Swiss viticulturist, crossbred many hundreds of White Riesling and Sylvaner vines at the Hessian State Research Station at Geisenheim between 1882 and 1891. His object was not to produce the finest grape variety in Germany, but to improve the quality of everyday German wine by combining the early-ripening, high-yield characteristics of the Sylvaner with the stamina and fine flavor of the White Riesling.

And he did just that. His success is reaffirmed each year by the great amounts of mild, flowery, pleasant table wine made from this variety in the Rheinhessen and Rheinpflaz, with sizable production also in Franconia, Baden, and Württemberg. Even along the very Riesling-conscious Mosel at least 10 per cent are Müller-Thurgau vines—mostly grown on the flat areas beside the river. Other European countries have recognized the forthright qualities of its wines, and sound Müller-Thurgau wines are now being made in Austria (Burgenland District), in Switzerland, in France's Alsace, and in the Alto-Adige, Trentino and Lombardy regions of northern Italy. Its most recent success has been in New Zealand, where it produces what may be that country's best commercial white wine—there called "Riesling-Sylvaner" or simply, but incorrectly, "Riesling".

When carefully made, the wine is clean to the taste and remarkably fresh and fruity. In some localities, and especially in certain years, its wines have a touch of muscat flavor or even a hint of nutmeg in others. Its primary deficiency is its usual lack of acidity. Only rarely should it be aged longer than two years in the bottle, simply because once the youthful fruitiness of the wine disappears, there is precious little left.

To give the variety its due, however, it must be said that, in poorer years, it easily surpassed in quality the other Riesling-Sylvaner hybrids and often performs even better than the Sylvaner. Its enthusiasts point out that in Germany it is generally listed third in importance behind the aforementioned varieties, and, while the vast majority of it is found in the less aristocratic and flatter lands of the Rheinhessen and Rheinpfalz, a claim to some noble status can be based on the fact that the first fifteen frost-prone meters, rising up the hill behind the Saar River's famous Schwarzhof, are planted to Müller-Thurgau vines.

If the story be without much glamour, it is not without mystery. It seems, curiously, that there are no remaining records of Dr. Müller-Thurgau's work, no definite proof to substantiate the theory that the variety is indeed a Riesling-Sylvaner cross. Most disturbingly, the flavor of the wine is quite unlike any other hybrid of those varieties, which makes the theory look shakier still. If that isn't enough material for doubt, we can add that all subsequent hybrid research has failed to duplicate the Müller-Thurgau's characteristics. So we are left with only two tenable explanations; first, that the combination of genetic factors which Müller-Thurgau synthesized from the Riesling and Sylvaner was a very rare one; or second, that the variety is not a cross at all, but a mutation (see glossary) of the White Riesling. At this stage of the game, with what little information we have, the choice is open.

Given the workhorse aura which surrounds this variety, and its flavor potential, it is revealing that few knowledgeable wine lovers will gainsay the possibility of vast improvement of Müller-Thurgau wines. The reason for this is its relatively recent "discovery" and extensive planting which prevent anyone from claiming with certainty that it will not produce superb white wines in its own right when enough time has passed to allow for the hit-and-miss selection of ideally suited vineyard sites, the same painstaking production processes which have already taken place with the White Riesling, for example. Once settled in optimum locations, the Müller-Thurgau will ultimately realize its potential, and, in something of an ugly duckling transformation, will surely surprise more than a few.

Certainly, it's a variety destined for further research—and probable rewards—in America. Professors Amerine and Winkler in their "California Wine Grapes" (Bulletin 794, published in 1963) and in their research as early as 1944, state that the Müller-Thurgau, because of its early-ripening, may well find a place in regions where other early-ripening grapes will not mature. In the variety collection at the University of California at Davis, the vine is vigorous and the fruit quality is excellent. All that is needed, of course, is the time and experimentation to place the wine in its ideal microclimate havens.

Traminer (Gewürztraminer)

plate 8

Traminer (Gewürztraminer)

Viticultural Profile:

The Traminer is a vine of moderate vigor and limited yield. Though its wood bears a sizeable quantity of fruit, the clusters are small (75-100 grams) and globular, thus limiting the amount of crop the vine can bear.

The semi-upright-to-trailing shoots are small with short internodes and bear leaves which are small, dull-green, rough in appearance, and generally three-to-five lobed. The cluster is small, round, and well-filled to compact.

The berry is small, oval, has a firm pulp, a tough, thick skin, and is unique in that its color at maturity is characterized by a russeted pink undertone with a nice trace of brown. As Traminer approaches maturity, its fruit is easily and pleasingly distinguished by a pronounced spicy flavor and aroma. The vine ripens early in the season, and often late-summer, high temperatures will decrease the delicate spicy aroma and give slight bitterness to the wine. Therefore Traminer is recommended only for the coolest growing regions—particularly, the cooler microclimates in California's coastal valleys and in the states of Oregon and Washington.

Generalities are leaky things, but it is true that most Gewürztraminers are frontal attacks on the senses. The aroma, texture, and flavor of a fine Traminer, or Gewürztraminer, create a stunning impression. These wines are at once soft and perfumed, but not subtle. The wine often seems less the product of the grape than of some Tolkien-like imagination or a tale of the Brothers Grimm. It is, perhaps, the most exotic of the great wine grapes—producing a fascinating, exciting wine of great flavor concentration. There is mellowness, originality, fullness and fire, all in pleasing proportion.

There is, however, an unnecessary confusion about its identity: Traminer and Gewürztraminer are one and the same grape variety. "Gewürz" (German) or "spicy" Traminer is simply the name applied to those strains of the vine producing more aromatic and distinctive wines. Since a strain of this more distinctive vine has been singled out through careful selection in the French Alsace, in Italy's Tyrol, in California and in fact in most regions of the world where Traminer is cultivated, there is little reason to quibble over which name is proper.

Traminer/Gewürztraminer may be so rich in varietal flavor that, if it can be faulted on any grounds, it is usually for a lack of subtlety. There is a positive side to this liability, however in the form of two interconnected major advantages. Being so distinctive, Gewürztraminer offers ready relief from the myriad of subtle, delicate (and often characterless) white wines; secondly, its pleasing assertive nature attracts the wine enthusiast not yet experienced in the subtle nuances or multi-faceted complexities of so many other wines.

Connoisseurs most certainly do not denigrate the Gewürztraminer for the forthright pleasures it offers. It is, without question, one of the world's most distinctive wines.

There are a few solid bets as to the origin of Traminer. One claim is that the variety was brought from the Middle East to Yugoslavia by traders during the Middle Ages. Its long history in eastern European countries such as Rumania and Hungary (where it is called the "Formentin") lends some credence to this theory. Yet a strong majority insists that the vine is native to the Italian Tyrol, specifically around the town of Termeno, south of Lake Caldaro. Before the Treaty of Versailles in 1919, this region was part of the impressive Austro-Hungarian Empire, and the town was called <u>Tramin</u>. Ties with Austria are still strong in these parts, reflected today in the modern winemaking equipment and techniques, relatively foreign to the greater part of Italy.

The three European countries to adopt the Traminer on a large scale are Germany, France, and Austria. Germany through the centuries has had a love affair with sweet, fruity white wines, directing its technological genius toward creating and perfecting fermentation and storage techniques that vinify this style of wine. The Traminer, with its tendency toward low acidity, residual sugar and a precocious fragrance, was the beloved of winemakers from the Rheingau to Baden-Württemberg throughout the 18th and 19th Centuries (even surpassing the revered Riesling).

The love affair came to an end with the discovery of the Riesling's more delicate flavor variations. When compared to the Riesling, the Traminer's singular, head-on taste labeled it a monochromatic fellow, lacking diversity. Plantings ebbed so drastically that today only a tiny fraction of the acreage in the Rheingau, Rheinhessen, and parts of the Palatinate is given to the Traminer. Its reduced dominions are the sandstone soils of outlying portions of the Palatinate, the Neckar River vineyards between Heilbronn and Stuttgart, and principally, the rolling terrain of Baden-Württemberg. The identifiable character of all the wines from all these regions is predicatably aromatic, leaning toward sweetness, sometimes rather common, and deficient in acidity. Often the Traminer is blended with these other wines to lend its lively fruity aroma to the less distinguished product.

In France, virtually all Traminer resides in Alsace, a strip of land near the Southwestern German border which for nearly 100 years was tossed about like a political hockey puck. Beginning with the Franco-Prussian War in 1870, Alsace has been under control of the French or Germans so many times that at present its spoken language is neither French nor German, though its heart is definitely French.

The three predominant varieties in Alsace are the White Riesling, the Sylvaner, and the Traminer. The vinification methods are fundamentally French—traditionally slow-fermentation to near dryness with minimal racking and filtration. Alsatian winemakers are nearly fanatical in their insistence upon natural winemaking techniques. The clear regional preference falls on heady, ripe, racey, dry white wines with higher alcohol content than the German counterparts. Such ideas have shaped the Alsatian Traminer. When grown in the most ideal climatic vineyard sites cradled between the Vosges Mountains and the Rhine River, Alsatian Gewürztraminers have come forth as the world's standard for this variety.

Whenever a champion is crowned, it is not long before a challenger throws down the gauntlet. As of now, the crown rests on Alsace. But, as with so many other classic varieties, the New World Gewürztraminers are beginning to be heard from. California has been working with this variety for no less than 125 years, ever since Count Haraszthy presumably introduced it in the 1850's. Until only very recently, the Traminer had been confused with a lesser, but vegetatively similar grape known as the Red Veltliner. This confusion along with the disruption caused by Prohibition impeded progress with Traminer wines. Obscurity is impossible for any such distinctive grape, so it is no surprise that California, along with Washington State and Oregon have made high quality Gewürztraminers, with the commendable dash, verve and the unique style so typical of the grape.

To repeat, happily for the wine enthusiast, no wine region is granted perpetual laurels. A good wine once made encourages a better one, and the New World contingent, especially in California, Oregon and Washington, is working hard to produce Gewürztraminers to rival any in the world. It is probably the most exacting variety to harvest at precisely the proper time; picked too early, its wines will resemble a Muscat; if harvested too late, the grapes, if not enjoyed by migratory birds, will yield low acid wines. In the last decade, California Gewürztraminers, as they are generally labeled, have evolved into a unique appealing wine: characteristically spicy in aroma and flavor, yet delicately balanced in residual sugar and acidity. Sonoma County and the Monterey-Salinas Valley have thus far spearheaded this movement, both in quality and quantity. But several finely crafted Gewürztraminers have already been made in the cooler Pacific Northwest states of Washington and Oregon. (Knowing Traminer as a vine of low vigor that performs best in the cooler districts, California has already developed a cross of Gewürztraminer and Sémillon called _Flora_, standing ready to be cultivated in climatic zones unsuitable for the tempermental Traminer.)

Australia and New Zealand have also felt the attraction of Traminer wines. The Australian State Department of Agriculture released its first bottlings in 1964; since then, acreage has steadily increased. The wines to date have proved commendable, though relatively short-lived and light. But their lineage is clearly evident in their clean, inimitable aromas and balanced flavors. New Zealand's efforts, as with so many other _Vitis_ _vinifera_ varieties there, are just now emerging from the experimental stages.

Wherever grown and vinified, the Traminer is always a tough customer for the producer. Its per acre yield is rarely in excess of four or five tons and usually much less; the pulpy nature of its berries further reduces the quantity of juice extracted. It will not perform well in warmer regions of the world, and as if all this weren't enough on the negative side of the ledger, birds consider the aromatic Traminer a gourmet delight and feast on the smallish clusters with a disheartening thoroughness.

But then again, no fine wines are made because it is easy to do so. For the winemaker, the question is, does the final product merit the effort put forth? In the case of Gewürztraminer, regardless of its different style, the question can only be rhetorical.

Chenin Blanc

plate 9

Chenin Blanc

Viticultural Profile:

Chenin blanc is a vigorous grower, yielding from four to six tons per acre in the coastal vineyards, and up to eight to ten tons in warmer California locations. It produces well when cordon-trained and spur-pruned; its canes are semi-erect and medium large.

The clusters are medium-large, long-conical and compact. The tender fruit is often subject to bunch rot. The leaf is three to five lobed, with a grayish-green color and distinctive red veins. The same pigmentation is present in the petioles. The berry has a rich, fruity flavor with good acidity. It is medium in size, oval in shape, and has a tough skin.

Though it is placed in the towering shadows cast by the noble French wine grapes—Cabernet Sauvignon, Pinot noir, and Chardonnay—the Chenin blanc (or Pineau de la Loire) has managed through a long viticultural history to present bright appealing wines — light, delicate, and refreshing. Curious, but these same appealing characteristics apply to the countryside that nurtured the vine through history: the Loire Valley, the Garden of France. With its pear, plum, and apple orchards, graceful strands of poplar along the Loire River and endless flowered meadows, the Loire Valley, not too surprisingly, was the summer residence of French royalty for centuries.

It was here that the Chenin blanc evolved its many styles. Springing from the first legendary fourth-century plantings of the vine by St. Martin on the north bank of the river opposite Tours, an entire family of distinct yet related wines have appeared, not only in the Loire Valley's Touraine and neighboring Anjou Districts, but internationally as well.

Probably the best know of all is Vouvray, produced in eight communes which share the French controlled appellation. Stylistically, it can be a dry, heady _vin de consommation_; a more studied, rich, honey-like wine labelled _moelleux_; or just about anything in between.

In great years, the grapes used in making the sweeter wines are infected with the mold _Botrytis cinerea_, the friendly attacker whose concentrating effects on grape sugar also produce Bordeaux's wonderful Sauternes and the berry selection late-picked Rieslings of Germany.

A third version of Vouvray is sparkling, made either _mousseux_ in the Champagne method, or only slightly so (two to three atmospheres per bottle) and called _pétillant_.

Similar to, but considered less fine than Vouvray, are the wines made across the river at Mountlouis, and those made at Jasnières about twenty miles farther north.

Fifty miles west of Vouvray, in Anjou, are the three other most celebrated areas cultivating the Chenin blanc. Exploring them, one occasionally hears the name "Blanc d'Anjou" replacing the more familiar one. The first stop is Savennières, which yields the lean, aristocratic, dry Chenin blancs. With their incomparable breed and intricacy, they comprise a category in themselves. Along the Coteaux de l'Aubance, on the south bank of the Loire and east, we find sunnier, sweeter wines; sleek and understated, tinged with _gout_ _de_ _terroire_ (taste of the soil). Still farther south is one of the real powerhouses of the Loire: the Coteaux du Layon. Here the best sites, such as Quarts de Chaume and Bonnezeaux, have their own separate controlled appellations, giving us the ripest, most supple and balanced Chenins of the region. Botrytised grapes almost always make up some proportion of the harvest.

Chenin blanc is also the only permissible white variety for the still wines of the Coteaux de Saumur. The well-known sparkling wines of that town need legally be only 40 percent Chenin blanc, allowing for the blending of more body into the very acidic wine.

For the sake of perspective, it is helpful to remember that all of these favored locales are surrounded by vast expanses of less noble, less specific appellations, most notably "Anjou-Saumur" and "Coteaux de Touraine". Almost 200,000 acres are accounted for between them, and naturally Chenin blanc is here blended with varieties of lesser quality, such as Chasselas, Arbois, and the Gamay à jus blanc.

Aside from being cultivated to some extent in the area around Bergerac where it becomes a remarkably unexciting wine, in France the Chenin has remained the exclusive domain of the Loire Valley. It is hard to believe, but notable plantings in other countries, with the exception of the State of California, are comparatively miniscule.

Another exception to this situation in Russia's Ukraine, where substantial acreage now yields above average, slightly sweet wines. On a lesser scale, both New Zealand and Australia have small plantings which may well expand in the future. But again, the big exception which is no secret to Americans is California, where the Chenin is something of a major producer. Starting out known as "White Zinfandel" and "Chablis" in the latter half of the 19th Century, it was not introduced under its proper name until 1955. The success of this venture can be measured by the fact that acreage has increased from a few hundred in Napa and Sonoma some ten years ago to close to 20,000 acres in 1976. The biggest plantings are now found in the Central Valley areas, in Monterey County, and in the established districts north of San Francisco Bay.

Today, other than finding numerous Chenin blancs on a store shelf, one is likely to find bottles made from this variety labeled "Pineau de la Loire" and even a few remaining known as "White Pinot". The latter is actually a misnomer, since the Chenin is a family of wine grapes unrelated to members of the Pinot family.

In California its most worthy efforts, both dry and sweet, and there are excellent examples in both styles, normally come from the cooler mountain and coastal vineyard districts. As contrasted with the blending wines produced from inland valley vineyards, these quality Chenin blancs maintain good acidity, offer clean fruity aroma and flavor, and solid character. Often, in fact, they surpass even their French counterparts in that ineffable fruity quality so central to their charm and wide appeal.

An added recent boost to the upward mobility of Chenin blanc in wine circles was the introduction of so-called "cold fermentation", in which fermentation takes place in temperature-controlled tanks. By slowing the rate of fermentation, the winemaker is able to preserve the fruity constituents which are usually broken down by a warmer and faster fermentation.

It is not overstating the case to say that formerly most Chenin blancs were branded "picnic wines" on the basis of their light and fruity, if slightly pedestrian, flavors. But with the advent of cold fermentation, the wines have climbed high in consumer appeal; even the most traditional connoisseur will admit, often with great surprise, that new dimensions have converted the picnic wine into a memorable feast.

Sémillon

plate 10

Sémillon

Viticultural Profile:

The Sémillon is a vigorous grower, and can be quite productive, when short or spur-pruned. It thrives on gravelly clay loam soils where, with irrigation, it dependably yields six to eight tons per acre.

The vigorous shoots grow semi-upright with large, round, roughened leaves. Usually the leaf is three-to-five-lobed. The large leaves provide the tender fruit with protection from intense sunlight.

The cluster is medium-large, conical, winged, with a thickened woody peduncle (see glossary). The berry is medium-sized, round, with a thin skin, and soft, juicy pulp. When mature, the berry develops a rich yellow color, and with more sun exposure takes on an amber-pink hue.

The Sémillon is a mid-season ripener and, when fully mature, the fruit develops a rich, fruity, almost fig-like aroma and flavor.

The fine white wine produced from the ripe Sémillon is admirably distinct by any standard. Sémillon can be made into either dry or naturally sweet white table wines, and under unique climatic conditions can be made into majestic, rich, sweet dessert type wines.

Enjoyable as it is, the dry Sémillon wine is just a small part of the reason for the variety's renown. The true miracle of Sémillon is to be found in its French homeland, principally in a small district in the Bordeaux region which gives its name to this special wine: Sauternes. Historical research indicates the Sémillon has been a principal vine in the Sauternes district since the First Century. Sémillon's name probably derived from "Saint Emilion"; possibly as an homage to the saint or perhaps taken from the Bordeaux district of St. Emilion where, strangely, no Sémillon is grown today.

The actual area of Sauternes' controlled appellation, located about 20 miles southeast of Bordeaux, is made up of five small townships: Barsac, Bommes, Fargues, Preignac and, of course, Sauternes itself. Each of these contains a number of chateaux producing wines under trademarked names. Most famous among them is undoubtedly Château d'Yquem, owned by the Lur-Saluces family. Its wines are masterpieces of delicate yet forceful sweetness, and have been praised over centuries with almost monotonous enthusiasm by everyone from Thomas Jefferson to the Czars of Russia.

For centuries, the tradition of blending compatible wine varieties has been common practice in all Bordeaux districts. For making Sauternes. the producers usually blend the Sémillon with about one-third Sauvignon blanc and a very small amount of Muscadelle to create the final product.

In the larger Graves district, a little north of Sauternes, the Sémillon comprises about one-third of the blend with the rest coming from the Sauvignon blanc to make the finer dry white wines. In Graves wines, the Sémillon is said to contribute softeness, body, and roundness, while the Sauvignon adds backbone, acidity, and aroma. But in the Sauternes district, in most vintages the climate enables the grape varieties to transcend their individual personalities, as all three grapes benefit from the effects of the mold, _Botrytis_ _cinerea_, or "Noble" Rot (_pourriture noble_), though the Sémillon is most susceptible to it and correspondingly more valuable in the blend. This mold acts in Sauternes exactly as it does on the Riesling grape in many German wine-producing districts (where it is called _Edelfäule_), i.e., it reduces the grapes' water content through the softening and piercing of their skins, thus allowing evaporation. The berry shrivels and its sugar content increases proportionately, and the acidity also increases. Fermentation is slow; finished alcohol, acidity and residual sugar, and intense honey-like flavor, to which the mold contributes, are high.

The involved procedure of harvesting the grapes is also much the same in both countries. Many separate pickings (anywhere from four to fifteen) are required each season, since only infected grapes are acceptable and the rest are left on the vine until they are rotten and fall off.

The delicious aroma and flavor of the resulting wine are as unusual and intense as they are impossible to describe. Rather than citing some secondary source, this writer suggests a good bottle of Sauternes as the best reference.

Sémillon has never performed a solo in its native France, being an important part of the blended wines of Sauternes and Graves.

When the Sémillon was recognized as a quality wine grape years ago, it was introduced into California. Unfortunately, it arrived during an imitative era in California viticulture. Thus it went into generic wines called "California Sauterne" (without the "s"). Some California Sauterne(s) were sweet, others dry, although in France "Dry Sauterne" is unknown. For the sweeter generic Sauterne, producers often added words like "Haut", "Sweet", or "Chateau" to denote high residual sugar.

Over the years, almost all of the useful distinctions have become blurred in California with respect to wines labeled "Sauterne". Some of them were not even made from the Sémillon. Fortunately, generic Sauterne wines seem to be gradually disappearing as varietally labeled wines replace them.

Progress in the production of varietal Sémillon wines has been considerable in California. One major problem, which may actually be a blessing in disguise, is that in general the less humid conditions do not encourage the development of the noble rot with Sémillon. However, there have been recent reports of its appearance on some Napa and Sonoma plantings of White Riesling, Sauvignon Blanc, and Chardonnay. To date, the only botrytised California Sémillon wine was induced artificially. But recent surveys from growers in the Salinas Valley in Monterey County offer encouraging evidence of the beneficial mold's appearance. We may be soon hearing of natural sweet California wines made from Sémillon grapes infected by botrytis.

If because of the absence of botrytis, the classical Sauternes flavor seems out of reach, still many attempts have been made to find compensatory factors for the lack of sweetness and concentration. For example, research has revealed that while the California north coast plantings often lack natural sugar content, and the inland valley plantings (around Kern and Tulare counties) tend to produce "burned" or "raisined" wines, the areas around Livermore, in Alameda County, and in the southern Salinas Valley, seems most advantageous, both climatologically and geologically, for full ripening of the Sémillon and the making of distinctive dry or semi-sweet table wines.

Though not so globally planted as the Cabernet or the White Riesling, the Sémillon has had auspicious beginnings not only in California, but in Australia (where it is often labeled as the Riesling), in Israel and in Chile. The variety has adapted itself typically well in each situation, but of course, the wines differ in style according to respective climates and vinification techniques. Chile, for instance, produces pleasant, drier wines resembling those of California's north coast counties, while Israel turns out wines in the heavier and sweeter category, but with less acidity.

Like other classic wine varieties planted the world over, the Sémillon produces wines which are more a spectrum than a single jewel. All retain something of the characteristic Sémillon roundness and depth—echos of Sauternes' greatness, if you will—but at the same time the basis for a whole gamut of the fine table wines unto themselves.

Sauvignon Blanc

plate 11

Sauvignon Blanc

<u>Viticultural Profile:</u>

The Sauvignon blanc is a vigorous producer, yielding from four to six tons per acre when the vines are fully matured. It shoots are semi-upright. Leaves are bright and grassy-green, three- to five-lobed; these are plentiful and provide good protection for the fruit from the sun.

The berries are small, round to short oval, and light-green in hue. Clusters are small, making them sometimes difficult to harvest; they are well-filled to compact, long-conical and often winged. At maturity, the fruit develops a rich characteristic flavor.

Among the first-rate classic white wine varieties, Sauvignon blanc cuts possibly a lower profile. In the eyes of most wine professionals, it falls short of the power of the Chardonnay and the grace of the White Riesling; somewhere in the recent years' quality shuffle in California its potential seems to have escaped full development.

The Sauvignon blanc is by nature powerful. Curiously enough, that is its potential tragic flaw. Its strength too easily becomes aggressive, indiscriminate and coarse as compared to the relatively harmonious and integrated power of the Chardonnay, for example. It is the bare-knuckle boxer rather than the master of karate.

I hasten to add that this description is usually applicable only to Sauvignon blanc wines which have been fermented to total dryness or apparently to those which have come from vines planted in heavy soils. The very dry wines lose the sleek, aromatic qualities obtainable from the variety, leaving it one-dimensional and slightly harsh. Those from heavy soils tend to mingle the distinctive varietal character with (some say) the smell and "taste" of that ground (gout de terroir), producing, to be blunt, an undesirable wine. The soil itself doesn't contribute, chemically, to this taste: apparently, its evil influence is in the vines' growth rate in heavier medium.

Through the centuries, French winemakers discovered two major stylistic approaches to their Sauvignon blanc, each in its own way circumventing these pitfalls. The first grew out of the variety's native region immediately south of Bordeaux, known as Graves; and the latter being adapted to conditions along the 400-mile length of the Loire Valley several hundred miles north of Bordeaux.

The strategy was to plant in the lightest possible sand and gravel soils, and to vinify so as to maintain a breath of fruitiness and sweetness in the wines. The Bordeaux show matador skills in preserving that bare wisp of amiable warmth couched in crystalline and austere acidities. The most famous Loire Sauvignons, those of Sancerre and Pouilly-sur-Loire (called Pouilly-Fumé) reflect these same qualities, though with the rounder, more gentle flavors one might expect from richer soils and inland weather.

The second method was also developed in the Bordeaux area, but still farther south, in the district called Sauternes. Here winemakers hit on the idea of tempering the Sauvignon's pungent character with the flowery, liquorous qualities of the Sémillon variety. When infected by Botrytis cinerea, (the famous benign mold (Pourriture noble) active in that region,) the Sauvignon blanc develops great firmness, depth and an intensity of flavor—almost smoky in nature—to which Sauternes certainly owes some of its great aging capacity.

Sauvignon blanc's California history began officially in the 1880's, though it had been cultivated to a small extent before that time. Mr. Charles Wetmore, a San Francisco journalist and founder of Cresta Blanca winery, obtained some cuttings of Sauvignon blanc vines, among others, from far and away the most famous Sauternes-producing estate in France, Château d'Yquem. Wetmore divided the treasure between his own holdings and those of the El Mocho Vineyards, later to become the property of Wente Bros.

In the gravelly loam soils of Livermore, with good sun and the tempering agent of San Francisco Bay nearby, the Sauvignon prospered. It showed a characteristic ability to adapt, and was soon producing (and still does) the most distinctive and full-flavored dry wines of its kind, better even than French wines of similar style.

But, in spite of its successes, it never really caught on, either with growers or consumers. Were the drier ones too heavy, shades of that bare-knuckled boxer again? The sweet wines, blended with Sémillon as in France, were delicious, but lacked the concentrating effects of Botrytis.

The Sauvignon seemed stalemated. Until the late 1960's it was practically left out of California's big wine boom. But it was then that it appeared under a new name — Fumé Blanc, a reversal of one of Sauvignon's Loire Valley names.

The wine was a master stroke, a product of the exciting experimental winemaking spirit of California wineries which has thankfully continued on into the Seventies. Crisp, clean, dry, yet strikingly fruity, Fumé Blanc is in some knowledgeable eyes the unequivocal equal of the finest Loire wines. It was provided the Sauvignon blanc with a new popularity and has greatly expanded plantings, most notably in Monterey County.

Palomino

plate 12

Palomino

Viticultural Profile:

The Palomino is a vine of such vigor and so fruitful that overproduction must be continuously checked by careful pruning. It thrives in hot climates: in California's San Joaquin Valley, the Palomino yields as much as ten to fifteen tons per acre. Grown in cooler coastal valleys, normal production is six to nine tons of fruit. This variety is best adapted to sandy loam or loam soils.

Clusters, loose to well-filled, are large, occasionally winged, and rather irregular in shape. The berries—pale, medium to large, oblate in shape—contain a firm pulp within a moderately-tough skin of greenish-yellow coloration which, when ripe, carries a heavy white bloom. The combination of thick pulp and tough skin creates both advantages and problems: the grape can survive, if nature demands, both early rains and excessive heat during harvest. On the other hand, its thick pulp produces a grievously low yield of juice.

The leaves are large, often with five lobes and dull, dark grey-green in color. Shoots are usually semi-upright, but sometimes trailing. Obviously, this variety is recommended only for California's warmer regions. In cooler climates, its extremely low total acidity becomes a liability and unfortunately, the must (juice) has a tendency to oxidize or brown easily, making this otherwise outstanding variety unsuitable for table wine production.

With the possible exception of the legendary vines of Noah's fabled Biblical vineyards, no grape enjoys greater historical significance than the Palomino. Its importance is intricately linked with the fame of sherry and the history of Jerez, the capital city of Spanish sherry trade. In southeastern Spain, these vines are known to have been cultivated ever since the Phoenicians founded the town over 1000 years B.C. Taken by the Moors in the Sixth Century, the capital city of the sherry district was named _Scheris_ by the Moorish hordes; it was reconquered by El Cid circa 1264; the name of the city, however, retained its Moorish flavor when it evolved into the more recent "Jerez de la Frontera." The Palomino—although the Moslem Moors forbade production of any alcoholic beverage—did not suffer from Moorish invasion. On the contrary, the vineyards were preserved as a source of fresh grapes during the entire course of the occupation; the Palomino is a delicious and sweet fresh fruit.

The English—after the Spaniards, of course—were the first of modern peoples to discover the vast potential of sherry. The word "sherry" is, in fact, an anglicized version of the wine's birthplace—"Jerez." During the Elizabethan wars with France, it became obvious that the tables of England—including the dining-board of Her Majesty—would become barren of the French clarets which had become the customary British dining beverage. The intrepid Sir Francis Drake, being of political bent and with a view toward maintaining the Queen's approving eye, instituted a quiet raid upon the Spanish coast at Cadiz (an enterprise which may have justifiably inspired the Spanish

Armada) and returned to the shores of England with 2900 butts of mellow sherry as cargo. Incredible as it may seem, sherry became a popular table wine of England and remains so today.

It is probable that the sherry which found its way to England was fortified with brandy for greater travel stability. It is also a matter of record that the British palates required a touch of sweetness to the otherwise bone-dry beverage. To the dry Palomino a sweeter wine was added, and the resulting blend became known as "Sack" or "Sherry Sack".

Men of state, men of the arts, men of letters soon learned to prefer sack: among them were Samuel Pepys, Isaak Walton and William Shakespeare. Shakespeare's own lovable man of girth, appetite and wit—the Great Falstaff—whose sweet tooth is known to all the world, was an outspoken admirer of the great wine of Spain.

Perhaps the Elizabethan preference for sherry was not new, even in the days of Good Queen Bess. In Chaucer's "Pardonner's Tale" there is a reference to this Andalusian wine. No wonder sherry has been called "the Englishman's wine." The Victorian writer, Anthony Trollope, expressed his own enjoyment directly when he wrote, "It seems to me that my dinner goes down better with a glass of sherry than without it." And it should be noted that the cellar books of Queen Victoria herself make frequent references to numerous bottles of Sack—for the Queen's table.

Immortalized as has been sherry in legend, song and lexicon of wines, one must give credit to the Palmino variety, which accounts for nearly 90 percent of the vines cultivated in and around

Jerez de la Frontera. The uniqueness of this grape derives from its response to the special climate and soils of its native district as well as the behavior of the wine in the Jerez environment.

Outside Spain, no producer has yet been able to duplicate exactly the particular characteristics of true sherry. It is true, of course, that a few American 'sherries' and one or two Australian and Argentine-produced wines, all made under "flor" yeast, are approaching "the real thing".

In the growing districts of Jerez, the Palomino is planted in highly calcareous soils which some experts believe somehow enables the grape to develop higher sugar content. To further this sweetness naturally, after harvesting the grapes are frequently laid out on mats to dry in the sun.

For centuries, the grapes were trodden by foot to extract the precious juice; today, however, the crushing and pressing have been mechanized for economic reasons.

Sherry makers often add calcium sulfate (gypsum) to the must to improve its acidity. This process is unappetizingly called "plastering" in the trade. Unappealing as it sounds, this additive increased acidity to a desirable level and endows the wine with the delicate, dry, crisp finish so typical of all "fino" sherries.

Fermentation of sherry is accomplished in quiet, cool bodegas (cellars) from harvesting until approximately the following January when a mysterious and wonderful manifestation occurs: yeast cells begin to form upon the surface of the new sherry in a strange design reminiscent of tiny flowers in full bloom. Hence, of course, this phenomenon is called "flor." The arrival of this condition is natural and spontaneous, yet no two butts, no matter how close together, develop the same degree of flor yeast character.

The two basic types of sherry are "fino" and "oloroso," both of which are made primarily from the Palomino. Finos are light and delicate, usually straw colored; olorosos are darker, smoother and richer due to their higher sugar levels. Olorosos are fortified (see glossary) early hence they have little or no flor character. To be genuine, an "amontillado" should be an aged fino, held in butt for from five to eight years. A "manzanilla" is special, the most delicate of all sherries, acquiring its superior qualities only when aged and matured at the sea town of Sanlúcar de Barrameda, once more proof of the Palomino's senstivity to subtle climate changes.

Manzanilla was unknown until the turn of the 19th Century when the solera system came into being. Simultaneously, the concept of a specific annual vintage date was eliminated, the necessity eliminated by the solera.

The solera system is constituted of a number of butts of a similar style arranged in tiers, forming a sort of inverted pyramid. As the oldest wine is drawn, the butts are refilled with a younger wine; the casks of younger wine are, in turn refilled with a still younger wine, and so on. This procedure occurs several times a year, basically a form of fractional blending assuring consistency of style for each sherry and thoroughly intermixing the flor yeast inoculum from butt to butt. Nearly all sherries are blends which may include wines of great antiquity together with wines of—say—five or six years (or less) aging.

It is probably relevant to point out that while virtually all Spanish sherries are made predominately from the Palomino grape, nearly all sweet sherries acquire their sweetness from a very dark, extremely sugary grape, the Pedro Ximenes, frequently dubbed "PX" in the trade. While only 10 to 15 percent of PX is necessary to change a dry Oloroso into a sweet wine, the rich, sweet sherries called Amoroso, Brown sherry, Cream sherry or Bristol Cream contain fairly large percentages of PX.

For many years, the Palomino grown in California was erroneously called "Golden Chasselas" or "Napa Golden Chasselas." For the knowledgeable purists, it is worthy of mention that there is a distinct but totally unrelated grape variety properly named Chasselas doré. This vine is called Fendant in Switzerland and its local name in Baden, Germany, is Gutedel. Chasselas doré is cultivated in Alsace and in France's Loire Valley near Pouilly-sur-Loire. It is also a widely used fresh table grape in France.

It is rather paradoxical that the Palomino, so tough in the vineyards, yet so sensitive to slight variations in climate, soil and vinification techniques, should be deficient as a table wine variety. On the other hand, this workhorse of sweltering vineyards is indispensible in the production of sherries of unsurpassed breed, delicacy and refinement. It is a study in contradictions.

Muscat Blanc

plate 13

Muscat Blanc

Viticultural Profile:

The Muscat blanc, doing business as Moscato di Canelli in Italy and Muscat Frontignan in France, may be described as a vine of below average vigor, depending upon soil conditions. At best it is only moderately vigorous in medium-to-fine textured soils—such as sandy loam and clay loam—but its growth habits on sandy soils demonstrate even less enthusiasm. Nourished properly on a suitable soil, however, it ripens well and can produce six to eight tons per acre in California's warmer districts.

The vine is semi-upright, its shoots carrying medium to large light green leaves which are lobed and sharply serrated. Typical clusters are well-filled to compact, medium-to-large in size, and when ripe are long, cylindrical and often heavily-winged. Individual berries are moderately large, round to slightly oblate; the ripe fruit develops a deep golden color. Expert observers describe its appearance as "oil-soaked" at full maturity. It has a very distinctive and pronounced—albeit delicate—muscat flavor.

This muscat variety is extremely sensitive to sunburn, a condition complicated by early to mid-season ripening. Severe crop loss and raisining of the fruit has been experienced by this variety in the warmer districts of California as a result of sunburn. Nevertheless, the fruit matures adequately in the cooler regions, and even those grown in warmer valleys produce well-balanced musts. Wherever it is grown, however, Muscat blanc must be regarded as a superior quality white dessert grape.

The muscat family is ancient, large, diverse and versatile. Although clouded in the mists of antiquity, there is evidence to support the theory that all the world's great wine grapes may be descended from some muscat variety discovered around the Mediterranean Basin by a Phoenician sea captain or a wandering Roman soldier who returned home (from the East?) with a few vine cuttings. Wine grapes change personality—and characteristics—when grown in different regions and coddled by different growers through centuries. Today one can find a Muscadelle du Bordelais, a Muscat d'Alsace, Muscat Otonel, Muscat Terracina, Muscat Saint Laurent, Muscat of Alexandria, Muscat Frontignan and Orange Muscat.

In spite of its ubiquity in Europe as a whole, the muscat is still heavily concentrated along the Mediterranean coastline, and it should be noted that not all muscats produce palatable wine. Some are better as fresh table grapes, others as raisins, but a few members of the family are triple-threats. This is a rare combination that few other grape families can claim.

No doubt the brightest quality star in the muscat galaxy is Muscat blanc (also known as Muscat Canelli and Muscat de

Frontignan). Traditionally—and what a tradition it enjoys!—Muscat blanc has been transmuted into a sweet, rich dessert wine. In a broader sense some of its dessert wines have been fortified (with brandy added to increase alcohol content), some have been made from the essence of sun-dried raisined grapes, and a few have been vinified as naturally sweet table wines. Italians love to make—and drink—sparkling muscat wines. In the late 19th Century, muscat brandy was a great favorite among the pioneers of California.

It seems quite natural that the muscat family should adapt to the rough and ready pioneer environment: it literally exudes strength of character and outspoken self-determination. In fact, it was the sole variety capable of maintaining its own unique characteristics and flavor when California researchers experimented with induced botrytis cinerea (the "noble mold") in a wide array of grapes. The only process that may have altered its disposition—slightly—has been the slow, gradual acclimation to a new home.

The Muscat is as rich in history as it is in flavor. Muscat blanc is also known in France as Muscat blanc à petits grains (white muscat with the tiny berries); it has been recognized by that name since the days of Charlemagne. It is the backbone of French muscatels and almost synonymous with viticulture in the Midi and, specifically, Frontignan regions of southern France. The northern Italians might well claim similar proprietary rights to this variety—known to them as Muscat Canelli. Produced for centuries in the mountainous Piedmont district, Muscat Canelli provides the essential soul of Italy's (and much of the world's) most popular sparkling wine—Asti Spumante.

In his book _Dionysius_, vine historian Edward Hyams reports that the Greeks established vineyards in the Crimea in the 6th Century with cuttings of their favorite grape, the _moscato_. It traveled from Byblia in Thrace to their colony in Syracuse and thence to their trade headquarters in the Crimea. Moscato wines were first mentioned in relation to Syracuse in 700 B.C. In nearby Noto, in Sicily, local inhabitants have been making and enjoying moscato wines for centuries.

Legendary Constantia of South Africa proffered a muscat wine known as "Constantia of the Cape." It was once highly esteemed and believed to have been produced from the Muscat Hamburg, or Black Muscat. Alas, it no longer exists. It left, however, a legacy. Late in the 19th Century, Australia was engaged in brisk trade with South Africa. Cargoes bound from the Cape to the land of the Southern Cross are conjectured to have included cuttings from the famous Muscat vineyards of Constantia.

Over the rugged Arrabida Mountains, about 20 miles south of Lisbon, lies a little town called Setúbal. Perhaps the most famous of all muscat wines, itself called Setúbal, is produced there. Hugh Johnson describes Setúbal as "the port of the Muscat world—an extraordinary concentration of grape flavour, the very essence of aromatic hot-house grapes." Sétubal is a fortified wine made by soaking the highly aromatic skins of the Muscat grape in the wine *after* it has fermented. A well-aged Sétubal is one of the vinous treasures of all fortified wines.

North of the Pyrenees mountains, which angle down to the Mediterranean coast between France and Spain, is France's most famous muscat region—Frontignan. The lovely wine of this region, also called Frontignan, is slightly fortified, very sweet, but yet delightfully delicate in flavor and fragrance. Frontignan prides itself as one of the several tiny pockets of muscat vines which are scattered throughout southern France. The wine villages of Lunel and Riversaltes vinify muscat wines in a style rather similar to that of Frontignan. The tiny village of Beaumes-de-Venise, just to the north of Châteauneuf-du-Pape in the Rhone valley, is worthy of a side trip to sample the local muscat wines.

Local winemakers in Sicily and its neighboring islands cling to the tradition of making muscat wines of tremendous concentration by sun-drying the grapes until they are almost raisin-like before fermenting them into a thick, delicious sweet nectar. Pantelleria, a tiny island, is best known for its fantastically beautiful full-bodied muscats.

In France, Spain, Portugal, Italy, Africa, Australia, Greece, Sicily and the Soviet Union, the muscat grape is justifiably held in exceptionally high regard by wine lovers. It was named centuries ago by the Italians: Muscato, in Italian, means *smelling of musk*. Musk is a secretion of the musk deer, a substance used in making the finest perfumes. Musk is found, too, in apples, pears and melons. It is said to be identifiable in the aroma of roses and definitely in the members of the muscat clan of grapes. The mingled aroma of perfume, roses and fruits would seem unbeatable in wines. And that, of course, gives muscat wines their incredible appeal—their highly distinctive scent.

Muscat wines enjoy popularity everywhere—except in the United States. Following repeal of the 18th Amendment, the Muscat of Alexandria provided the source fruit for the cheap fortified wines associated with the skid rows and alcoholic down-and-outers who haunted America's twilight zones. The word muscatel became synonymous with social downfall.

As a result, there are fewer than 800 acres of Muscat blanc grown in the United States, most of them recently planted in the Interior Valley of California. Muscat of Alexandria, although more extensively cultivated in those hot regions from Fresno through Bakersfield, is harvested to a large extent for raisins.

During the American wine boom, muscat wines remained in limbo. But a new awareness is beginning to sweep away superstition and an unfortunate past history. As connoisseurs continue to cultivate a taste for sweet wines, muscats are once more gaining popularity. And winemakers—having at their disposal the finest equipment for controlling fermentation temperatures, are collaborating, applying their technical talents to both Muscat blanc and Muscat of Alexandria. Through the magic of controlled fermentation and proper viticultural practices, several exotic versions of light, sweet Muscat blanc wines have been made in California. These wines have captured the superb delicacy of aroma and flavor intrinsic to Muscat blanc together with a proper balance of acidity and sweetness.

One long-established producer in the Napa Valley has gained laurels for his limited production of an extremely long cold-fermentation of Moscato Amabile which is light, delicate and delightfully "petillant," or slightly sparkling. Several other wineries are presently producing most attractive sweet sparkling wines in the style of Asti Spumante.

There are signals, according to enologists at the University of California, Davis, that muscat wines—particularly varietals created from Muscat blanc—are divesting themselves of their earlier poor image. The experts believe—and rightly so—the Muscat blanc will become one of California's finest wines.

Delaware

plate 14

Delaware

Viticultural Profile:

A vine of moderate vigor, the Delaware performs best in deep, gravelly well-drained soils where it will produce up to 6 tons per acre. Its small, slender canes are semi-upright to trailing in appearance, and for optimum fruit quality, careful pruning is required.

The moderately three-lobed leaf is small to medium in size, light green-yellow on the upper surface, with occasional russeting on older leaves. The anterior surface, also, is light yellow-green. Berries are small, round to short oval in shape, pink to bright red at maturity. Their pulp is quite juicy, almost gelatinous in consistency, with a most distinct fruity flavor delightful to the taste when fully ripe.

Developed clusters are rather small, often shouldered, globular, somewhat cylindrical in shape, making harvesting a painstaking and comparatively slow process. The fruit reaches maturity in New York state about two weeks before the Concord, thus escaping the danger of early frosts; in fact, this grape achieves full maturity in most growing regions.

And, of vital importance to growers in the eastern United States, Delaware can survive cold winters.

U. P. Hedrick, probably America's leading grape authority at the turn of this century, in 1908 described the Delaware as "the (Eastern) American grape _par excellence_." At that time, it was "next to the Concord, the most popular grape for garden, vineyard and wine-press...grown in the United States."

Delaware—which was not named after the state bearing the same melifluous nomenclature—was brought to prominence by Abram Thompson, editor of the Delaware (Ohio) _Gazette_. During the summer of 1849, when the cream of American manhood yearned to saddle up and ride for the gold fields at Sutter's Mill, Thompson turned his back on the temptations of Californ-eye-ay, and instead kept a close watch on the grapes that came into Delaware from the outlying farms. Especially the bright pink-red variety cultivated on the farms of Mr. Warford and Mr. Heath, two of the local gentry who farmed some acreages a few miles from Delaware on the Scioto River. Thompson sent some of the fruit to A. J. Downing, the horticulturist and landscape engineer who designed the gardens for the White House; Downing gave the grapes the name of Delaware—in honor of the town from which they had come—while Thompson, in turn, brought his grapes to the attention of the Ohio Pomological Society (in 1851).

Although the vine was traced back to origins in New Jersey, the trail became increasingly misty. Theories were advanced that it was a true _vinifera_, but the idea was abandoned. Whereas at least one viticulturist put forth the suggestion that it was of labrusca-Bourquiniana origin with a touch of vinifera, another (Millardet) expostulated that it could be a hybrid of vinifera, labrusca, cinerea and aestivalis.

If the Concord is celebrated for having provided American grapegrowers with an early burst of enthusiastic vigor, the Delaware must earn credit for sustaining and improving that drive for many decades. In gauging the quality of any eastern American variety, the Delaware must be held up as the benchmark. In the garden, it is admired for its beauty, its delicious flavor and luxuriant growth.

Philip Wagner, owner of Maryland's Boordy Vineyards and retired editor of the Baltimore Sun, wrote in all seriousness that it is "difficult to resist growing lyrical over this lovely fruit. It is small and delicately formed, pale rose in color, with a bloom of greyish lavender, and it grows in bunches that are plump and voluptuous: it is the finest of all our white wine grapes, by general agreement." And the late Frank Schoonmaker, one of the sternest critics of all wines and grapes, eulogized the Delaware in these terms: "This peerless fruit is one of the brightest jewels in the crown of American viticulture."

Today, the Delaware stands first in rank among the high quality native American grapes. Like many of its distinguished coadjutors, it is challenging to grow, temperamental and sensitive to the various slings and arrows of survival— insects, mildew and robins, which, by the way, feast upon it at every opportunity.

Like Shakespeare's melancholy Prince, the Delaware is

perhaps a little schizoid. It is classified as a red-fruited variety (actually the color is closer to pink), but its juice—like that of almost all wine grapes—is white.

The Finger Lakes district of New York is the primary adopted home of the Delaware. Total acreage is not huge by any means, since the Concord still represents more than 50% of the total New York production. But such figures do not reflect reliably the value of the grape. At the turn of the century, when brigades of the WCTU assaulted the bastions of the Demon Alcohol, the Delaware was indicted and condemned as a wine grape, whereas the Concord was accorded gentler position as a table grape.

In spite of its somewhat small yield, today the Delaware is one of the few native American grapes that develops excellent sugar content for winemaking, often exceeding the 22% level. Its acidity, however, is variable. To experience the truly unique flavor of pure Delaware, one should really taste one of the unblended Delaware varietal wines currently on the market. As Philip Wagner has said, the Delaware "sails proudly under its sprightly bouquet and delicate flavour."

Outside the state of New York, the Delaware is grown in several regions. There are small plantings in Michigan, Arkansas, Pennsylvania, Missouri and—of course—Ohio. In the past decade these growing areas have been revived to join the wine Renaissance in America.

In the interim, much has happened: Plantings of French-American hybrids have been encouraged in the eastern

United States, however most Americans, it would seem, are leaning toward vinifera wines . . . leading one to wonder what might have been the fate of the Delaware, if it had not been singled out for destruction by proponents of Prohibition. Had the Eighteenth Amendment not enjoyed such longevity, and had it not left such keloidian scars in its wake, Delaware might well have experienced a better fate after Repeal.

But rather than dwell upon what might have been, it is better to remember that the recognized authorities in the field of native American grapes and wines appraise Delaware as one of the best.

Catawba

plate 15

Catawba

The historic Catawba (of mysterious origin) is a vigorous and productive variety with sufficient hardiness to resist the severe winters of the eastern United States. The vine thrives equally in sandy, gravelly or clay-loam soils, especially where there is good drainage.

Ripening later than other _Vitis labrusca_ varieties, it is sometimes necessary to cluster-thin the vines and to encourage sun exposure. Clusters are well-filled to compact, medium to large in size, and nearly cylindrical in shape. Berries are large, oval, and dull purplish-red with a lilac-colored bloom. The skin is thick but variable in relative toughness, low in pigmentation—making it only slightly astringent—and demonstrates the typical _labrusca_ 'slip-skin' characteristic.

The Catawba leaf is most distinctive: large, entire to moderately three-lobed. The upper side is medium green, rough and leathery; the under surface is wooly-white with dense tomentum (see glossary).

Many early experts recorded the flavor of this fruit as mildly "foxy"—a term used to describe the aroma and flavor of the Concord—as well as uniquely 'grape-y' and aromatic. Berries ripen one or two weeks later than either the Concord or Delaware, which makes it a problem child in regions with a limited growing season. Obviously, it must be restricted to the warmest sites.

Unlike the irrepressible Mr. Bull's Concord, no one has yet unravelled the mystery of Catawba's origins. It is well documented that a vine called 'Catawba' was introduced in 1823 by John Adlum, a nurseryman of the District of Columbia, who obtained cuttings from a Maryland farm in 1819. The woman who originally owned the vines, a Mrs. J. Johnston, who lived near Fredericktown, Maryland, told Adlum that her husband had always called the grapes 'Catawba,' but she had no idea when or where they had come from.

A German priest, after having tasted Adlum's grapes, solemnly pronounced them to be exactly the same as the Tokay of Hungary, whereupon Adlum began to call his vines by that name. Several years later, however, he discovered that the nomenclature was erroneous, and—with much embarrassment, it is presumed—he went back to the Catawba name. Exactly why the grape was called Catawba in the first place is still a mystery. Catawba was the early name given the Wateree river, which joins the Congaree to form the Santee river in South Carolina. Dr. U. P. Hedrick, a grape authority who conducted in-depth research on the Catawba shortly after the turn of the 20th Century, reported in his tome, "The Grapes of New York State," published in 1908, that John Adlum's correspondents, who lived in South Carolina a century earlier, seemed never to have heard of the variety.

The Catawba yields a wine of rugged individuality—admired by many. At one point in time—between, say, 1825 and 1850—it was the most popular grape grown in the United States. While it gave way to the Concord, which could perform better, even in regions with shorter growing periods, it has never plunged into obscurity. With its iron constitution, it continues to maintain its present position as one of the most prolific grape varieties cultivated in the eastern United States.

The Catawba vine was introduced into vineyards near Cincinnati by Nicholas Longworth in 1825. As soon as his cuttings bore sufficient fruit, the famous early wine grower began producing white Catawba table wine and sparkling Catawba...which were sold as far afield as California and brought still further fame and fortune to the diminutive winemaker. Thanks to Longworth's efforts with Catawba vines, Ohio was the leading state in winemaking by 1859—producing about a third of the total national volume. The Ohio River valley was known as "the Rhine of America."

A corresponding journalist from the _Illustrated London Times_ flattered white Catawba table wines as "a finer wine of the hock species...than any hock that comes from the Rhine." With equal expansiveness, he proclaimed that Sparkling Catawba "transcends the Champagne of France." At about the same time,

America's unanointed poet laureate, the hallowed Mr. Longfellow, rhapsodized over Mr. Longworth's vintages in his "Ode to Catawba Wine," to wit:

"Very good in its way is the Verzenay
Or the Sillery, soft and creamy,
But Catawba wine has a taste more divine,
More dulcet, delicious and dreamy.
There grows no vine, by the haunted Rhine,
By the Danube or Guadalquiver,
Nor island or cape, that bears such a grape
As grows by the beautiful River."

Among poetic purists, Mr. Longfellow must surely have dropped some of his laurels with his attempt to rhyme "River" with "Guadalquiver," words which have no phonetic similarity whatever.

Obviously the sensitive ear of Bacchus was offended: only a few years later, the Catawba vineyards in Ohio were decimated by _oidium_, the powdery mildew and other fungi, blasting the infant industry before preventive measures were yet discovered. By the 1860's, most of the vineyards "by the beautiful River" were totally destroyed. Susceptibility to fungi constitutes the main defect of Catawba, which explains its sudden decline. Late ripening, which severely restricts its cultivation, is of course its other drawback.

Nevertheless, even today the Catawba remains the leading grape variety along the shores of Lake Erie in Ohio, and it plays an important role in the present-day vineyards of New York's Finger Lakes District. Restricted as it must be, due to late ripening, the Catawba now accounts for less than 10% of the Finger Lakes total wine production, although the vine enjoys plantings in Michigan, Arkansas, Georgia, Pennsylvania, South Carolina and Missouri. "Catawba Pink," the most pleasing rosé version created by Charles Fournier, one of the world's leading wine and vine scientists, undoubtedly has led to increased plantings. Mr. Fournier always used Catawba in his finest New York State 'champagne.'

Although generally classified as a _labrusca_ variety, it is difficult to pin down the Catawba within a precise species. The vine resembles a _labrusca_, but many authorities believe it reveals _vinifera_ blood-lines through its rather strange susceptibility to various fungi and mildew. A Californian may claim that Catawba wines are characterized by the unique aroma and flavor known as "foxy;" to an eastern winemaker, those are fighting words. Most eastern enologists who have worked closely with the grape, however, maintain that it has a delightful and distinctive aroma and a flavor somewhat reminiscent of a _vinifera_. Disposing of those opposing points of view in a cavalier fashion, it is probably more honest to say that the Catawba is a native American grape that may have picked up some _vinifera_ parentage along the way.

Lightly pigmented, Catawba is suitable for white table wine, sparkling wine or rosé. Planted in better locations, it develops fairly good sugar content; on sites where maturation is late, the Catawba rewards the grower with good acid balance. With utmost diplomacy, Philip Wagner, a distinguished wine author and proponent of French hybrids in America, commented that Catawba wines "more or less resemble the Moselles." So be it.

It is doubtful that the Catawba will ever again rise to the heights it once achieved in American viticulture; but it is still a very important grape for winemaking as well as a delicious table grape. Critic, remember: it was honored as the first native American wine to be given serious national and international recognition, the first full-fledged ambassador of the American wine industry. Catawba has well earned its place among the great wine grapes of the world.

Aligoté

plate 16

Aligoté

<u>Viticultural Profile</u>:

The Aligoté is a good producer that is capable of yielding four to seven tons per acre. Of average vigor, it produces best when spur-pruned.

The clusters are small to medium and compact. They are conical in shape and often winged. The leaves are three-lobed to entire, thick and dark-green. They are glabrous above and slightly tomentose below. The petioles have a reddish-purple hue.

The berries are round to oval in shape, and small in size. When mature, they have a gelatinous consistency, giving them something of the "slipskin" characteristic which is common among native American grapes.

The Aligoté variety is rarely represented as more than a footnote in the story of wine. In general quality, it could conceivably be ranked alongside of the Sylvaner, but it is not as widely cultivated, more often blended, and, therefore, doubly less in evidence than its German counterpart.

Its origins are French, and its history solidly Burgundian, harkening back to better days when it was planted alongside the

Chardonnay and Pinot blanc on the Côte d'Or and in the Chablis district. Long since banished from these sanctums, it is now found with the Gamay on the top and reverse side of the Burgundian Côte, on the flat plain between the slope and the river Saone, and in other areas of less favorable exposure and soil composition.

The resultant wines, along with those Aligotés of the French Chalonnais and the Mâconnais, are permitted to be labeled "Bourgogne Aligoté", "Bourgogne Ordinaire", or "Bourgogne Grand Ordinaire"—nothing more specific. These include the best of what the Aligoté has to offer. Most are medium-bodied; all are dry. The greater part of them have a curious crisp edge and a rather abrupt finish: however, occasionally one runs across a bottle with some nicely married flavors and an uncomplicated smoothness. Ordinarily, aging beyond two years is inviting disappointment.

What is surprising about the Aligoté in the rest of France is not the quality of its wines, which is rather low in most départements, but just how far afield it can be found. The quantities are never awesome, it is true. Still, it is actually easier to enumerate those areas in which it is not cultivated than to mention those in which it is. From the Poitou to Lorraine, from the Touraine to Haut Savoie, virtually every wine-bearing region in France counts some Aligoté among its blending lots.

The exceptions to the rule are those areas with Mediterranean situations, where climatic conditions destroy even the modest level of quality attained by wines of more northerly origin.

Rumania and the Soviet Union are the only other countries of the world to fully accept the Aligoté. In the former it has been planted in the massive Focani vineyard of the central eastern area, while in the Soviet Union it is plentiful throughout Moldavia, the Crimean Peninsula, and elsewhere. In both countries it is often bottled under its proper name, but still contributes to blended dry wines and, less frequently, to the more traditional sweet ones.

In the Western Hemisphere, California is the sole commercial cultivator of the Aligoté, and even her interest has amounted to little more than a passing nod. In the early sixties there were no more than sixty acres planted to it, most of them in the North Coast counties. A decade later, after a great boom in planting, that figure had not changed appreciably.

It seems reasonable to surmise that, in a land blessed with many prolific and inexpensive white wine varieties, the Aligoté was redundant. It simply cannot produce wines distinctive enough to warrant its planting over that of more easily cared for and more productive varieties. So it was bound to succumb to the effects of this "Law of Natural Selection" in California viticulture, as have other minor European vines imported more in the spirit of experiment than anything else.

Mission

plate 17

Mission

Viticultural Profile:

The Mission vine is vigorous, strong, and productive. A late ripener (late September to late October), it often yields twelve to fourteen tons per acre in warmer climates. The strong vines develop large trunks with strong drooping or trailing canes.

The leaves are large, dark green, sometimes with a reddish-purple hue, three-to-five-lobed, glabrous above. The clusters are large (one to one and one-half pounds), long-conical to irregular in shape, loose to well-filled. The fruit can resist mold and rot when remaining on the vine after ripening. The berries are medium-size, round to oblate, reddish-brown to reddish-purple in color, and have a pleasant strikingly fruity flavor with firm texture.

As is sometimes the case with great men in history, the fame of the Mission grape variety is less a matter of its real merits than of its being at the right place at the right time.

The right place was Spain (or so runs a widely accepted theory of its origin), and the right time was the 17th and 18th Centuries, when Spain had risen to pre-eminence as a world maritime power and claimant to a large portion of the "New World". The combination of factors catapulted this modest variety into great renown as the dominant, in fact the only, _Vitis vinifera_ (Old World) variety grown in California for over 125 years. The same variety, or one closely related, held the same position in Mexico for well over 200 years.

Mission's origin is still disputed, because, like the Zinfandel, for many years it was a _vinifera_ grape thriving in the New World while no examples of its type could be found in its native Europe. It was an orphan—at least until inquisitive viticulturists got around to looking for its parents.

F.T. Bioletti, distinguished early Professor of Viticulture at the University of California at Davis, formulated the most reasonable theory to date: the Mission is a clone, or possibly an old seedling selection of the Spanish variety _Monica_, with which it shares many biological and taste characteristics. It was probably brought to Mexico in the time of Cortez. It definitely prospered, possibly cloned or mutated, and was re-named _Criolla_. Evidence exists that plantings crept northward until it was being cultivated by Franciscan priests, in what is now New Mexico, around the beginning of the Seventeenth Century.

During the following 200 years, the Franciscans' role in the spread of Mission variety plantings was so primary that it is difficult to overplay.

Certainly one of the best indications of the variety's importance to the friars is the name it bears today. Their need for wine as a sacramental specie, and secondarily for table consumption, made it an indespensable and integral part of the mission system. Where they went, inevitably went cuttings of the wholesome, hearty, palatable and dependable workhorse called Mission.

The Mission (or at least a Criolla type) found its way to Baja California in 1697, planted at San Francisco Xavier Mission near Loreto by Father Juan Ugarte. Seventy-two years later, in 1769, it was planted in California soil, at San Diego, by Father Junipero Serra. Very successful subsequent vineyards sprang up at San Gabriel, Santa Barbara, and other Northern California sites, but an important fact emerged as the fathers moved farther and farther north: the Mission grape needs an exceptionally warm climate to ripen properly. Hopeful little plots at Santa Clara, Santa Cruz, and San Francisco had to be abandoned, and viticulture in Northern California became nearly dormant until the middle of the nineteenth century.

At that time growers hesitantly began again to plant extensive vineyards in the north. Fears of the great blight of phylloxera then raging in Europe, coupled with a great success of Mission in the south, led them, strangely enough, to include a preponderance of Mission vines. The classic European _vinifera_ varieties, better adapted to cooler climates, quickly showed their superiority, however, and the switch-over from Mission to these newcomers (the "great" wine grapes) was nearly complete by 1870. The only exceptions at that time were the Mission vineyards in the foothills around Los Angeles which were producing a very sweet, fortified wine called _Angelica_.

Today in California, the Mission is used primarily as a blending grape in fortified wines because of its high concentrations of sugar (24–28 degrees Brix), but low color and acidity. It is planted almost exclusively in the San Joaquin Valley or in California's Region V, defined as the hottest locales for viticulture according to the University of California heat summation chart.

Logically, the heaviest concentrations of Mission-type vines are in South America; notable in Argentina where the best-known is _Criolla de Vino_, and in Chile, where it is named _Pais_. There are more than a few clones prospering in these countries, and the wines produced vary greatly according to climate. In Chile's southern regions, where it grows without irrigation, the _Pais_ makes a rather bland but fair red wine from relatively well-colored fruit.

When one reflects on its history, Mission definitely has more "firsts" than "bests". It has been said that as a table wine the only things it lacks are color, flavor, and acidity. One might well ask how much more there is to wine.

On the positive side, Mission has taken part in that marvel of hit-and-miss and trial-and-error empirical development through which each variety finds a place for itself, some optimal way of contributing its best characteristic to the world of wine. Mission has performed a very real function, and is appreciated for it.

Zinfandel

plate 18

Zinfandel

<u>Viticultural Profile</u>:

Zinfandel is only a moderately vigorous but heavy producing variety. It crops quite dependably when short-or spur-pruned . . . six to ten tons per acre on good soils in California.

Shoot growth is trailing to open-prostrate, and fruit exposure to the sun is a common problem. The leaves, dark green in color, are deeply five-to-seven-lobed with a distinct lyre-shaped petiolar sinus.

The cluster is medium to large, cylindrical and heavily winged. It can be very compact. The berry is medium- large, round, thin-skinned, with a characteristic rust-colored scar at the apex.

The fruit ripens in mid-season, and is therefore often high in maturity with sunburned or withered berries scattered through the cluster. Wines high in alcohol often result from this condition. With early fall rains, berry cracking can occur and bunch-rot can be a serious hazard.

When fully ripe, the fruit develops a very pleasant, rich, berry-like flavor.

For more than 100 years, research viticulturists believed that Zinfandel had no traceable lineage. Until the late 1960's when it had become the second most widely planted red wine grape in California, the only known fact was that it had European origins since it had been classified as a member of the _Vitis vinifera_ (Old World) species. But inconclusive theories and claims were plentiful, casting the vine as something of a mystery and chimera in wine history. In _The Wines of America_, Leon Adams, the wine historian, reported that Zinfandel was nursery-grown as "Zinfindal" at Salem, Massachusetts in 1848, and earlier, on Long Island, New York, in 1830 as "Black Zinfandel," presumably (and probably) from Hungary.

There was nothing more illuminating than that, until the recent developments surrounding a chance discovery in 1967 by Dr. Austin Goheen, United States Department of Agriculture Plant Pathologist. Visiting Italian colleagues in Bari, Italy, he found this hithertofore orphan variety planted widely (over 75,000 acres) in southeastern Italy. There it is known as the "Primitivo di Gioia." Gioia is a town and district in the southern province of Puglia which covers most of the heel of Italy's boot. The greater part of the Primitivo grown in this warm climate produces a thick, heavy-bodied, red wine used mostly for blending purposes. However, at the nearby village of Bari, a distinct red wine resulting from careful vinification and extensive small barrel aging, demonstrates the breed and flavor intensity of the full-flavored, rich Zinfandels produced in California's cool coastal microclimates.

In 1968 Primitivo vines were brought from Italy and, after quarantine index testing, planted in the experimental vineyards at the University of California, Davis campus.

Starting in 1972, viticultural comparisons with California Zinfandel have been made, and the two vines appear identical in all respects. The Italian imported vines bore crops in 1975, and in all aspects, the fruit and the wine appear identical as well. More comparative wine studies will be made over the next few years.

Researchers have discovered through their investigations that the vine grows in Hungary and also in Yugoslavia, where it is known as the "Plavac" or "Plavina." By either name, it yields a medium-bodied red wine with Zinfandel's characteristic fruity aroma and flavors.

But as to how Zinfandel first journeyed to California, experts are still confined to speculation. The vine may have accompanied other vinifera varieties by way of Cortez' Mexican expeditions, and later have followed Father Junipero Serra (in the mid-eighteenth century) as he established his missions and vineyards along the California coast. It is more probable, though, that Zinfandel may have arrived in California vineyards through the pioneering plantings and entrepreneurial struggles of the fustian "Count" Agostan Haraszthy, the 'father of California viticulture'. The Count sensed something special about it when he wrote in 1864, "one day the Zinfandel will rival the great clarets of France." In this astute observation, he was only about 100 years ahead of his time.

Between its arrival in California in February of 1852 and the subsequent rapid expansion of Zinfandel plantings through the 1860's, it gained considerable quality recognition. By 1884, it was the most widely cultivated red wine variety throughout California, serving as the predominant wine base for California's numerous "Clarets". Many of these wines proved so pleasing that they demonstrated for the first time that truly fine wines could be produced in America.

Having named the illegitimate infant, wisely adopting it, and launching it so auspiciously, California vintners somehow continued to underrate and misunderstand its capability. Lacking any royal ties, it was considered as a less than noble variety, one that would grow anywhere. And it was planted everywhere, often in very marginal locations. Nobody viewed it as more than a fruity, light "vin de consommation", much like the Gamay grape of French Beaujolais. If aged at all, Zinfandel went into giant old redwood tanks; in the wineries, it was attended to only after the more important wines were pampered. But the situation, as well as the wine, is a good deal more complex.

Zinfandel is bewilderingly flexible. Grown in different locations and climates, it yields different wines. Some are light and fruity; others medium-bodied and balanced, others are dark, intensely fruity, and highly tannic wines that improve in the bottle for years. A few small wineries specialize in Zinfandel wines; many others are just as proud of their Zinfandel as of any other wine they make.

Wine aficianados have become aware that Zinfandel, (that "everyday Zinfandel" which has played and is playing such a key role in making America a wine drinking nation) when grown on cooler slopes in California's coastal counties and given all the personal attention normally reserved for the classic wines, can in fact yield wines that are full-flavored and tannic, distinctly berry-like in aroma, and capable of developing further nuances with cellaring. Planted in suitable regions, trained and pruned properly, carefully vinified, allowed to remain in contact with the skins after fermentation for a time, followed by periodical racking, cask aging, and bin aging…in short, if made by the same techniques applied to the making of a superb Cabernet Sauvignon, Zinfandel will reward winemakers (and all of us) by becoming a wine of regal proportions, with great style, unique character, and a powerful bouquet. In the cellars of many wine connoisseurs today, it is not unusual for bottles of Zinfandel to be aging alongside of prestigious bottles of Cabernet Sauvignon, and top-drawer wines from famous Chateaux.

Cabernet Sauvignon

plate 19

Cabernet Sauvignon

<u>Viticultural Profile:</u>

This variety is very vigorous but only moderately productive. With long- or cane-pruning it bears dependably up to five or six tons per acre on the good soils of California's coastal valleys.

The vine grows with strong, spreading, semi-upright shoots. The foliage is dark green when mature, and glossy green when young. The leaf is medium to large in size, deeply five- to seven-lobed with a deep-cut, open petiolar sinus, showing exposed or naked primary veins where they join the petiole.

The cluster is medium to small, long conical and loosely-filled. The berry is small, round, tough-skinned and heavily pigmented. Maturity is late in the season and the tough, small berries withstand unfavorable weather and resist spoilage to a high degree.

When mature, the fruit develops a characteristic pungent, aromatic flavor.

By common consent of studious wine drinkers, and by many expert witnesses among viticulturists, the four finest red table wine varieties in America are the Cabernet Sauvignon, the Pinot noir, the Zinfandel, and the Merlot. Of these, the Cabernet Sauvignon is overwhelmingly preeminent—unsurpassed in richness of flavor, intensity of bouquet, and longevity in the bottle. It has given American wines a position alongside the very great wines of the world.

France's Bordeaux districts are recognized as the Cabernet Sauvignon's home as well as its major showcases. Certainly, the superb clarets produced by the renowned chateaux of the Médoc, Graves, St. Emilion, and Pomerol districts are the epitome of excellence. Great red wines take time to evolve—years to discover the right varieties, years to match them to the suitable soil and climate conditions, and time to develop vinification techniques that can achieve maximum results. Bordeaux has devoted centuries to the Cabernet family.

During the Roman epoch, when Bordeaux was part of south Gaul, Pliny the Elder (A.D. 23-79) described a vine remarkably like the Cabernet. He called it Biturigiaca, after the Bituriges Ubriaci tribe which then inhabited the region. Columella, whose early description of the clusters, leaves, and vine structure was so extraordinarily accurate, shortened the name to Biturica. Centuries later the same plant was referred to as vitis dura, which was contracted to La Bidure and Vidure, one of the local Bordeaux synonyms for Cabernet Sauvignon.

This remarkably adaptable variety produces excellent wines in many countries: Bulgaria, Italy, Yugoslavia, Hungary, Rumania, South Africa, and Argentina, to name a few. The finest Chilean reds are also at least partially Cabernet Sauvignon;

Chile has more than 50,000 acres in cultivation. Australia grows a moderate amount of quality Cabernet, but is perhaps most proud of its internationally recognized Cabernet-Shiraz blends. Neighboring New Zealand, a late-starter in cultivating the classic variety, now has a limited amount of Cabernet Sauvignon, and has recently implemented an experimental program in which several lots of Cabernet have shown remarkable quality levels.

Although the basic Cabernet character manifests itself in wines from different countries, one should not compare their tastes competitively. The location of the vineyard, the conditions of the soil and the climate, vinification methods, aging procedures, and storage conditions all contribute to a wide range of regional styles and various nuances in aromas and flavors. And furthermore, the percentage of Cabernet used in the traditional blends heavily influences the final style and taste. For example, the great Bordeaux reds, though basically similar, reveal differences due, primarily, to blending practices and the preferences of individual winemakers. According to experts, Château Lafite is two-thirds Cabernet Sauvignon and one-sixth each of Cabernet franc and Merlot. Château Mouton Rothschild is 90 percent Cabernet Sauvignon, with 5 percent Cabernet franc and 3 to 4 percent Merlot. Château Haut Brion is 55 percent Cabernet Sauvignon, and 22 percent Cabernet franc, with 23 percent Merlot. In the chateaux around the village of Pauillac, the wines average 75 percent Cabernet Sauvignon; in the Graves district, 50 percent; and in the St. Emilion-Pomerol-Fronsac regions, 20 miles east of the city of Bordeaux, 33 percent. These percentages vary slightly from year to year, but always manage to present intriguing and exciting taste differences.

In California's coastal counties near San Francisco, the finest Cabernet Sauvignons rank among the world's greatest red wines. Most of these are 100 percent Cabernet, or nearly so. But in recent years, Merlot is being blended in more and more for added softness, roundness, and character. In California, the vine is quite vigorous, yet produces moderate crops on the deep rich soils of the valley floors. This happy combination of high vegetative vigor and lower productivity yields high quality fruit. In the noble varieties, huge crops and high quality are rarely, if ever, compatible.

The Cabernet is a miserable failure in California's San Joaquin Valley, and paradoxically, does very poorly in the extremely cool coastal areas. Extremes of temperature do not suit its temperament. Hot climates destroy its varietal character, producing wines unbalanced, and unpleasant. In the coolest areas, the variety does not ripen fully, giving a green (under-ripe), thin, and very astringent wine.

When a "big" Cabernet is produced, meaning one that is destined for a long, majestic lifespan, the young wine has a weedy or herbaceous character, almost bitter from its aggressive astringency. It takes an experienced taster to sample a Cabernet and predict its future accurately. It demands oak aging and time in the bottle as well. As it ages, it softens and further develops and extraordinary varietal character—warm, rich, full, rounded, complex, subtle, and altogether superb. Words are rendered inadequate to describe its bouquet, charm and style.

There are two additional Cabernet varieties which should not be confused with the Cabernet Sauvignon. First, the _Cabernet franc_ is an important variety of the St. Emilion district where superb wines are made.

In the Loire Valley of France it is the predominant red grape type, producing light reds and rosés. California's Ruby Cabernet (a cross of Cabernet Sauvignon and Carignane) is a pleasing, prolific variety created by geneticists at the University of California, Davis. It possesses less body, flavor, and distinction than the pure Cabernet Sauvignon. As of this writing, the university announced the imminent release of two new Cabernet crosses which are suited for cooler climates. A committee of Napa Valley winemakers claim these offspring to be as rich in flavor as the great one. As of now, one of these new California crosses, named "Carmine," is being highly tauted.

But for the moment, the Cabernet Sauvignon is the undisputed potentate, one of the world's, and certainly America's greatest red wine variety.

Merlot

plate 20

Merlot

Viticultural Profile:

The Merlot vine is a moderately vigorous grower, but consistently bears good crops. It has semi-upright shoots, deep green foliage, and leaves that are deeply indented with five to seven lobes. In general appearance, it is reminiscent of Cabernet Sauvignon. Long-or cane-pruning is recommended.

If left unchecked, Merlot has a natural tendency to be prolific. Growers normally prune it to reduce crop size and then, if necessary, later thin the clusters down to the desired yield for maximum quality. The medium-sized cluster is long and conical in shape, considered to be well-filled, but not compact. The berry is short-oval, medium in size, thick-skinned, well pigmented, and blue-black in color at maturity.

Having good productivity and being relatively disease-resistant, Merlot is capable of yielding eight or nine tons per acre, but thoughtful growers reduce its productivity to the four to six tons per acre range for maximum fruit quality. Viticulturists classify Merlot as an early-midseason ripener, whereas Cabernet Sauvignon ripens in the late season.

Expert viticulturists consider the Merlot to be one of the old, distinct _Vitis_ _vinifera_ varieties. Yet it has, over centuries, experienced many ups and downs. Certainly it is now one of the primary varieties in the production of great Bordeaux red wines, second only in importance to the Cabernet Sauvignon. It is believed the latter was not crowned king of the Bordeaux red wine grapes until after the vineyards were planted following the devastation of phylloxera (1860-1880). Vineyards planted to Merlot were thriving in the Bourg and Blaye districts, across the river from Margaux long before the Médoc vineyards were established.

One of the great injustices of the wine grape world may be that Merlot's pedigree pales slightly only when compared with Cabernet Sauvignon. The latter, though producing majestic wines, happens to be a tough, hardy vine, capable of withstanding most climatic viscissitudes, including late season rains and hailstorms. Merlot also produces wines which mature earlier than those of the Cabernet Sauvignon; and long-lived wines were cherished by the British, the major admirers of Bordeaux wines until a few decades ago.

Yet through the shifts in tastes and the reconstitution of vineyards, certain general patterns have developed in recent years. Merlot is more important in the red wines of the Pomerol and St. Emilion Districts of Bordeaux, while the Cabernet Sauvignon is the major variety grown in most of the famous Médoc vineyards.

Basically, (but with considerable variance) the average blend in a Médoc wine consists of about 1/3 Cabernet Sauvignon, 1/3

Cabernet franc, and 1/3 of Merlot. Another variety used sparingly but felt to be important is Petit Verdot.

The exceptions, though, are often more revealing than the generalizations. The famed wines of Château Petrus, Premier Grand Cru, in Pomerol consist of about 90 percent Merlot, and the equally regarded Château Cheval Blanc of St. Emilion uses about one-third Merlot. Both Château Haut Brion and its neighbor across the street, Château La Mission Haut Brion, contain approximately 30 percent of Merlot in their blends. Both are located in the Graves district of Bordeaux. And Château Palmer, a small but highly esteemed Medoc estate, is known to use around 60 percent of Merlot.

In Bordeaux, Merlot then is a blending wine, but a highly important one. At Château Lafite, for instance, Merlot is a most important factor. At this world-famous château, Merlot is fermented separately, and later blended with Cabernet Sauvignon and Cabernet franc. How much Merlot is used depends largely on the conditions of the particular vintage and the quality of wine the winemaker believes is possible under those conditions. In certain years, Cabernet Sauvignon may fall short of expectations, either failing to mature fully or becoming overripe. Merlot, by virtue of ripening earlier, is often used to contribute certain sensory qualities that this specific Cabernet may lack. At this juncture in the vinification, proprietors and wine masters make delicate decisions based upon years of experience and intuitive skills.

In most years, Merlot is said to contribute softness and roundness to Cabernet wines. It can counterbalance both the harsh tannins and the generally high natural acidity of Cabernet Sauvignon. Furthermore, Merlot has an herbaceous cabernet-like aroma. As a compatible wine with Cabernet, Merlot endows the blend with excellent fruit along with the harder to define qualities of "grace" and "finesse."

For all of these reasons and because of its good productivity and the relatively early maturing of its wines, Merlot has been more widely planted throughout Bordeaux in the last few years. Here it probably will always be a component of a blended wine labelled under the name of a château under a regional name in Bordeaux. The prestige of Bordeaux has been founded on this vinification philosophy: change is rather unlikely.

The region that focused attention on grape varieties and which may have as much to contribute to a superior quality appreciation of Merlot (as it has already with Cabernet Sauvignon) is California, the home of varietal labeled wines (along with Alsace—1920-1940—and Italy's Piedmont district). Merlot has been waiting in the wings while Cabernet Sauvignon yielded the fabulous red California wines that has brought it fame. As an understudy, Merlot suffered for years as a victim of inattention and vineyard and winery trials. The first studies of Merlot placed it on a "not recommended" list, faulting it for a lack of acidity and a delicate bouquet when grown promiscuously in California. Now, with the benefit of hindsight, one suspects that the trials were based on overcropped or poorly located Merlot vines and a failure to understand the individuality of the grape. But the viticulturalists followed these initial reports with subsequent trials in the 1950's and mid 1960's. These later investigations, though tentative, recommended growing Merlot in the cooler coastal valleys, with some reservations. But the need was felt for a wine to blend with Cabernet Sauvignon, and of all the compatible grapes, Merlot was finally deemed the most promising.

The door was opened: the wondrous and bold philosophy in California winedom now is that anything is possible through study, innovation, and experimentation. This attitude, combined with increased consumer interest in table wines, led to pioneering efforts with Merlot. By the late 1960's, a few patches of Merlot were planted and wines made in California in the north coastal counties, and producers began tabulating reactions of consumers. The feedback demonstrated positive reponses, and Merlot, once neglected, suddenly became the object of overwhelming interest. As new, cool wine growing regions opened in Monterey and Santa Barbara counties, and as established regions were expanded, Merlot vineyards were set out at an astonishing rate. Between 1970 and 1976, the acreage of Merlot increased 40 fold.

As these new vineyards come into production, California vintners will continue to experiment with the wine. A score of wineries have been using judicious amounts of Merlot to blend with their Cabernet Sauvignons. Several others have offered varietal

Merlot wines; some of these have been 100 percent of Merlot, while a few have been predominantly Merlot but with small percentages of Cabernet Sauvignon. The early indications are that wineries are convinced of the benefits of Merlot as a blending wine to offset the slow maturing property of Cabernet Sauvignon and to add complexity to the wines. Whether Merlot will stand alone as a varietal wine remains to be seen. In the next decade, California growers and winemakers will be learning more, and as the industry grows, Merlot seems likely to grow with it.

By virtue of its late start in California, Merlot has received the benefits from the great wealth of viticultural knowledge around the world. Greater attention has been paid to matching the variety with suitable micro-climates where it can perform classically. Today in the international wine community, vintners freely exchange information, since they all are trying to make the best wines possible. Today Merlot—because of its attributes— flourishes in almost all of the world's major vineyard regions.

Merlot is one of the few great wine grapes in the world which has no variant names. It is widely grown in Italy, especially in the northern parts of the country, and in the ancient Alto-Adige district in Trentino, is one of the outstanding red wines of that region, much in demand by Germans and Swiss. In Veneto, Merlot yields a slightly lighter wine than in the districts farther south. Overall, in Italy it is the fifth most popular wine grape. In another ancient wine region, Slovenia of Yugoslavia, Merlot has long been a favored red wine.

Outside of Europe, Merlot has traveled widely with great acceptance. In Chile, it is often found growing in vineyards south of Santiago; often, it grows alongside the Cabernet Sauvignon. The wines made from both noble varieties are indisputably the finest from Chile. Argentina is another major wine producing country. Merlot is found in those vineyards located around Mendoza. Much of the wine produced in this district is enjoyed within the country with the emphasis naturally falling on palatable wines for everyday consumption.

The Australian wine industry has many curious parallels with that of California. Down under, scientist and university researchers work closely with the vintners. In 1966 the Barossa Valley winegrowers worked through the Department of Agriculture to select the best wine grape varieties for its climatic variations. After an extensive investigation, six wine grapes were singled out for improving the quality of Australian wines; among these was Merlot. Not too far away in New Zealand, scattered plantings of Merlot can be found as part of experimental projects. Wherever interest in wine is keen, Merlot seems to be playing an increasingly important role.

Despite its rather anonymous but important nature in famous Bordeaux wines and its delayed but encouraging debut in California and other major winegrowing regions, Merlot may come to be recognized soon (if it is not already) as one of the five top red wine grapes in the world. Cabernet Sauvignon and Pinot noir surely rank supreme, but not too far behind one could easily place

Merlot. At least a very strong argument can be made on the basis of Merlot's involvement to some degree in so many of the world's most sought-after red wines. Then again, we have yet to hear the closing arguments, since California may demonstrate to the world before too long that Merlot can unquestionably stand by itself as a regal varietal wine.

Pinot Noir

plate 21

Pinot Noir

<u>Viticultural Profile:</u>

The Pinot noir is only moderately vigorous and is low in productivity. On good sites in the coastal valleys of California, with long- or cane-pruning, it can bear as much as four to six tons per acre. At four tons, the fruit is usually more mature and higher in quality. The crop ripens quite early and sunburns easily, which is liable to give an alcoholic, or even a raisin-like character to its wines.

The vine of Pinot noir has an open, sparse appearance with shoots semi-upright to trailing. The clusters are small, cylindrical, winged, and well-filled to compact. The berry is medium in size, oval, deeply pigmented and contains many seeds.

The leaves are bright green, somewhat roughened and distinctly three- to five-lobed.

Drs. Maynard A. Amerine and Albert J. Winkler, two of the world's leading wine and vine scientists, wrote, "The true Pinot noir is one of the unmitigated joys of the experienced taster . . . It has a distinct and penetrating taste . . . a definite silky texture . . . among the dearest wines known, possessing a smoothness which by comparison makes some of the other great red wines of the world seem rough . . . , wines of great breed and distinction, great power."

Although some very good, and even a few great Pinot noirs have been grown in cooler climates in California's Napa and Sonoma Counties, the great 'breed' mentioned above applies almost exclusively to the 100 percent Pinot Noir wines produced and bottled in the old French province of Burgundy. To be more specific, the finest examples have been produced in the département of the Côte d'Or (the slope of gold), a thin, 40-mile north-to-south strip of superb vineyards beginning just south of the city of Dijon and continuing south to the charming village of Chagny. This advantageous southern slope (in latitude as far north as Washington State) provides the required sunlight exposure, climatic conditions, and well-drained soils for this temperamental, early-ripening variety. In other famous wine areas, such as Germany and Switzerland, the Pinot noir, true to its sensitive disposition, often fails to ripen sufficiently to produce full, dry red wines. Genetically, Pinot noir demands that all growing conditions be at their optimum.

Early botanists recorded accurate descriptions of Pinot noir as far back as the 1st century.

The invading Romans, often inclined to remove their vinous competition, actually encouraged the vine's expansion and wrote of its luxuriant wines. In the 15th century, the reigning Duke of Burgundy, wanting absolutely no competition from less qualified varieties, formalized the Pinot's supremacy by banning the Gamay grape from the northern Burgundy district, though it was hardier and more prolific. Today, however, some Gamay is still grown in the Burgundy district. Blends of the Pinot noir and the Gamay must by law be labeled "Bourgogne-Passe-Tout-Grains" (pronounced Pahss-too-gran) and must contain at least one-third Pinot noir. The great Burgundies—and they are fabulous—of Gevrey-Chambertin, Vosne-Romanée, Aloxe-Corton, Beaune, Pommard and the other famous wine villages of the Côte d'Or are produced solely from the Pinot noir variety.

Among its other outstanding contributions is its importance to Champagne. In France, approximately two-thirds of all Champagne is made from the Pinot noir, which has a "black" skin but a white pulp. When crushed, the deep, dark-purple skins are immediately removed and the white "must" (fresh juice) is fermented into white wines which are meticulously blended mostly with Chardonnay, into the cuvée or "lot", which is the secret of each producer. Pinot noir's flavor and its early-ripening characteristic—producing a proper degree of sugar and a somewhat higher acidity—make it the ideal Champagne variety.

A little-known "still" (non-effervescent) red Pinot noir is produced around the village of Bouzy in the Champagne District. Labeled simply "Bouzy", it is scarce, expensive, high in acidity and light, with a typical Champagne bouquet. Also, a smaller amount of light, delicate Champagne is made exclusively from the Pinot noir's illustrious colleague, the Chardonnay. This product is usually labeled "Blanc de Blancs"—white wine from white grapes.

The early quality reputation of the Pinot noir led to its being planted in many other countries—in Germany, Switzerland, Austria, Hungary, Rumania, Northern Italy, South Africa, Chile, Australia, in the north coastal counties of California, and most recently, in Oregon and Washington. In Germany (in the Ahr Valley near Bonn), it grows at a latitude as northerly as that of Labrador and produces red wines, which are rather pleasant, yet vague and mild, certainly no rivals to the great Burgundies of France. The original Pinot noir cuttings were brought from France to Germany by St. Bernard de Clairvaux, a Cistercian, some time early in the 12th century. In Germany today, the variety is known as the Spätburgunder or Rotclevner; it is also the principal red wine grape of Assmannshausen, immediately north of Rüdesheim, and also of Affenthal in the historic Black Forest near Baden-Baden. Of more interest is "Dole," Switzerland's best red wine, from the Canton of Valais, produced principally from the Pinot noir. It is a full-bodied, rich red, with good aging potential.

In America, along the West Coast, the Pinot noir has yet to demonstrate its greatness. From time to time, it has yielded really fine wines which, however, are lighter in color than their European prototype, yet demonstrating the typical 'nose', softness, and delicate texture. But these are the exceptions, not the rule. Hugh Johnson writes that the Pinot noir produces a rather common wine in California and likens it to a light Rhone red.

Truthfully, until very recently, the Pinot noir has received only a lukewarm recommendation from American viticulturists. But at the same time, research continues to find the best clones for specific locations in California, and the innovative winemakers are directing much of their efforts toward improving Pinot noirs.

As a genetically weak and sensitive vine, the Pinot noir presents numerous complications. It is one of the earliest-ripening varieties grown on the West Coast, and unless harvested rapidly, it tends to become over-ripe fast. Also, in the past, Pinot noir vineyards in California were plagued by virus diseases imported with the original cuttings from France. It is a vine of low vigor, and usually produces insufficient leaf coverage to shade the delicate fruit from the California sun. As a result, the California wines usually have less color intensity that one would wish.

Confronted by the challenge, the University of California remains optimistic that the Pinot noir will eventually take its rightful place beside the other great wines whenever the vine is grown under optimum conditions. This involves keeping the yield extremely low, cultivating the virus-free stock, planting in the finest microclimates, picking at optimum maturity (not overripe or sunburned), and fermenting slowly at ideal temperatures. Until these conditions are fulfilled as best as possible, however, it may not be possible to evaluate the product of this thousand-year old treasure in its transplanted home. We are for now left guessing whether someone, at some time, somewhere in California might just find the key. It is true, and encouraging, that, sporadically, "great" Pinot noirs have been made in California.

Gamay Beaujolais

plate 22

Gamay

plate 23

Gamay Beaujolais

Viticultural Profile:

The _Gamay Beaujolais_. For reasons explained later in this segment, the little black Gamay Beaujolais might well be designated as the "fruit of embarrassment." In the vineyard—due to cluster size, berry size and shape, leaf characteristics, pigmentation and wine aroma—this fruity, tart grape is difficult to distinguish from the Pinot noir. No wonder. Because it is indeed a clone (see glossary) of the Pinot noir, and should not be confused with a completely distinct variety variously called Gamay, Gamay noir or Napa Gamay.

Well adapted to California, when grown there the Gamay Beaujolais is a bit more vigorous—and somewhat more productive—than the traditional Pinot noir. Under circumstances of ideal location and climate conditions, this variety displays good berry set and produces an average of 4 to 5 tons of fruit per acre. The vine is usually long- or cane-pruned. Shoots are strong and upright, with long internodes.

Like its clonal relative the Gamay Beaujolais has three-to-five lobed leaves, medium in size, glabrous above with grooves at the veins, dark green in color. Berries are black, small oval in shape, with thin, tender skin subject to damage during harvesting. This fruit has a tendency to ripen a few days later than other clones of Pinot noir. Clusters are small to medium and heavily winged. The peduncle, tough and sturdy, is likewise dark green. It is interesting to note that the clone, Gamay Beaujolais, has small, light brown seeds, whereas the ancestral _Pinot noir_ boasts large, plump light-brown seeds.

Gamay

The _Gamay_, also known as the Napa Gamay in California, has moderately vigorous growth habits, but is very productive—capable of yielding 8 to 10 tons per acre in California's coastal valley vineyards. In fact, in cooler locations, its crop must be reduced by cluster thinning in order to obtain ideal maturity.

Large roughened leaves develop on the semi-upright shoots. In late season, the vine often acquires a somewhat undesirable openness which occasionally exposes the fruit to excessive sunlight. The well-filled to compact clusters are large, conical and heavily-shouldered. The berries are large, round and moderately tough-skinned. Unless this grape achieves optimum ripeness, pigmentation tends to be low, producing wines deficient in color. Ripening occurs in late midseason under ideal conditions, although in cooler regions full maturity is often difficult to attain.

"How can it be," you might properly ask, "that two varieties as viticulturally dissimilar as the Gamay and the Gamay Beaujolais could have been so seriously confused—and to some degree, still are?" Such confusion is not entirely incomprehensible. Bear in mind two factors: first, that the Burgundy district in France is noted for mixed plantings and numerous local grape names. Second, European wine grapes were exported from France to California at _different_ _times_. Certain Gamays were established in vineyards south of San Francisco Bay; others were planted in parts of Napa and Sonoma Counties to the north. While the southern vineyards enjoyed great success with a variety labeled Gamay Beaujolais, the northerly vinters cultivated a grape they called "Napa Gamay."

Quite naturally, it was assumed that these fruits were basically the same, attributing the differences in viticultural aspects (and the resulting variations in wine quality) to variables in soils and climates. French _vignerons_, for reasons of (a) disinterest in johnnie-come-lately American wines, (b) vast distances and (c) lack of definitive information, offered little help. Wasn't it enough that in Burgundy there are both red and white Gamays, and even a very unique Gamay with deep red juice? (This fruit is called _teinturier_ because the additional color is used as a blending agent to increase color intensity of light-colored red wines.) Additionally, the French producers very simply assumed that in the region south of Mâcon, called Beaujolais, the principle grape under cultivation was the Gamay Beaujolais, and that was that.

This blissful state of enological innocence would have continued had not American wine-bibbers developed a widespread taste for California wines called Gamay Beaujolais. In 1946, immediately following the conclusion of World War Two, the French government—beginning to feel the pinch of a growing American demand for American wines—politely requested that California wineries discontinue using an appellation which rightfully belongs only on wines made in the delimited Beaujolais district.

The Californians replied, through the voice of wine historian Leon Adams, that Gamay Beaujolais has been determined by ampelographers to be a distinct grape variety. Checking their own ampelographies, the French were embarrassed to realize that the reply was indeed true, and that the American winemakers were simply using a varietal nomenclature.

Neither the French nor the Californians, however, came out of the Gamay caper flying victory banners. The California wine industry, feeling a premature flush of success, asked Professor H.P. Olmo of the University of California, Davis, to settle once and for all the question of the relationship between Gamay Beaujolais and Pinot noir. The noted viticulturist concluded that the Gamay Beaujolais and Pinot noir are clones of the same varieties. He determined also that the variety known in California as the Napa Gamay is in fact grown widely in the Beaujolais region under its local name of "Gamay noir a jus blanc," a black Gamay with white juice. In the Beaujolais district, Gamay Beaujolais and Gamay noir (or Napa Gamay), are grown together, the latter used in making the light, fresh and fruity red wine enjoyed in its youth as _vin ordinaire_. Furthermore, the Gamay Beaujolais is probably used in making the longer-lasting Beaujolais wines, "Beaujolais Villages" and the nine top _Grand crus_ of Beaujolais which have their own appellations, Morgon, Brouilly, Côte-de-Brouilly, Chenas, Chiroubles, Fleurie, Juliénas, Moulin-à-Vent, and St. Amour.

Faces in the Beaujolais District remained red for a long time. It was especially painful for the vignerons to recall the famous edict of Philip the Bold of 1395 which forbade the cultivation in Burgundy of the Gamay grape, which was described by regal decree as the "_tres mauvais et tres desloyaux plant nomme gamay_" (the very evil and very disloyal plant called gamay). Confusion is an acceptable condition, but disloyalty in wine production, to any Frenchman, is an intolerable violation of the French heritage. In commenting about the royal condemnation of the Gamay, the French wine lexicographer, Dr. Gerard Debuigne, wrote wryly, "Fortunately for us, Philip's subjects were not entirely obedient."

On this side of the ocean, the California producers were not celebrating in self-righteous joy. They, too, had some problems, especially those enhanced by the fact that their marketing patterns had been established prior to clarification of the Gamay identification matter. Gamay Beaujolais had become a very popular wine; to reverse the field and call it _Pinot noir_ would be tantamount to making a single platter of _paté de foie gras_ from the goose that laid the golden eggs. Those unfortunates who regarded the Gamay or Napa Gamay a somewhat inferior third cousin of the Gamay Beaujolais were distressingly enlightened to learn that it was one of the true Beaujolais grapes, fully entitled to bear the authentic "Gamay of Beaujolais" escutcheon.

To say the least, confusion has been rampant ever since. Producers resist changing the name of the successful Gamay Beaujolais to the somewhat better known (in America) Pinot noir. Those who have been suffering under the illusion that Gamay is an underling are suddenly promoting their wines as similar to French Beaujolais. One can only hope that future labels will reflect the true grape variety used to make the wine. In California today, there are about 5,000 acres of each variety under cultivation. Gamay is dispersed throughout the state's vineyards. Gamay Beaujolais, a heat-sensitive early-ripener and a moderate bearer, is more confined to suitable locations such as the cool counties of Napa, Sonoma, Monterey, San Benito and Santa Barbara.

An interesting sidelight offering optimism for further identification of the two Pinot noir clones: University of California experts have long recognized the differences between the two grapes. In training enologists, they have stressed the characteristecs unique to each. At a convention of enologists in 1958, a paper was delivered documenting the long-held suspicion that Gamay Beaujolais and Pinot noir were clonal relatives, although closer scrutiny of these related vines has subsequently revealed small but distinct differences in viticultural behavior.

Wine-tasting experts can readily notice the subtle differences between the two resultant wines, even when the grapes are grown side by side. In the long run, it is probable that scientific knowledge and pervading common sense will eliminate the present confusion in nomenclature.

It should not be disturbing when differences become discernible; such differentiations are consistent with our present knowledge of clonally-related selections within a given variety. Gamay Beaujolais and Pinot noir have been proven to be members of the same family, but we may rejoice that each has its own singular personality. Those less concerned with technical accuracy may be delighted to know that there are not two, but _three_ different wine types: Gamay Beaujolais, Gamay, and, of course, Pinot noir. Such diversity is a most important reason for studying wine.

Grenache

plate 24

Grenache

Viticultural Profile:

The Grenache is a very vigorous vine which has a habit of being an "alternate" bearer. This means that for instance one year it is capable of yielding around eight to ten tons per acre, and on the next, it might produce around fourteen to sixteen tons on suitable sites. It is a late-midseason ripener, prone to rot and a withering blight called "deadarm," when the weather conditions are cool or damp. With thick, sturdy, upright growth, it is best spur-pruned with either cordon or head training.

The clusters are large, and well-filled to compact. They are short conical in shape, sometimes shouldered or winged. The berries are small to medium in size, oval to almost spherical in shape, and reddish-purple to black in color.

To the average American, Grenache is that deliciously delightful rosé wine which, when chilled, goes so will with a picnic lunch and a bright summer's day. Ever since its commerical inception in 1941, Grenache rosé has become the perennial favorite in the United States, which is the greatest public relations program the grape could hope to have. But as more and more people experiment with the world's wines, they are discovering just how much more there is to the Grenache story.

The Grenache is believed to be a native of Spain, where it flourishes today under the name "Garnacha". It is greatly favored for table wine production in Spain's Rioja Valley and Catalonia, and it is not hard to understand why, when one considers how few varieties can produce as perfumed and mellow a wine in such sweltering heat.

Its tragic flaw, a deadly one for a red grape, is its lack of pigment in the skins. This compels most wineries to grow it for rosés (pink wines), or to call it a "blending grape" and match it with something darker and more robust, such as Carignane. Paradoxically though, the same deficiency makes is terrifically versatile. The Grenache is an ingredient in a whole raft of different types of wines throughout the world—red, white, rosé; table and fortified.

That versatility is most evident in France, where it contributes heavily to the great bouillabaisse of wine from the Mediterranean regions of Roussillon, Languedoc, the Southern Rhone Valley and Provence. Known as Grenache, Alicante or Carignane Rousse in these parts, it is found in the lists of permissible blending varieties for most of the area's controlled appellations. The number of varieties entitled to a particular appellation will vary in each case from two or three to fifteen, but production from a single variety is unknown here. Generally, in this climate no grape can by itself produce a truly satisfactory wine;

whites are too often flat and without charm, reds harsh and dull.

Provence's best names, Palette, Bandol and Cassis all owe something to the softness and aroma of Grenache, as do the lesser V.D.Q.S. bottlings (Vins Délimités de Qualité Supérieure) of the Coteaux d'Aix. As a relatively light, mild and beneficial tempering influence in the wines of Châteauneuf-du-Pape, Gigondas and the Côtes du Rhône (including over 100 communes), it is becoming more popular than ever. Whether the entrepreneur likes it or not, drinkability is the keynote in wine marketing, and these stocky, barrel-chested red wines of the lower Rhone and Provence are becoming streamlined with ever greater doses of Grenache.

The Rhone Valley's benchmark rosés, those from the sandy soils of Tavel and Lirac, are the wines which provided the model for California's efforts. These owe one of the greatest debts to Grenache, regularly containing over 60 percent of the variety — as well as solidity and fullness not found in many a "good" red wine. Though far above the average in "Grenachness" they cannot claim its highest content. That distinction belongs, curiously, to a white; the strange golden fortified wine of the delimited area of Rasteau, which is required to include at least 90 percent Grenache.

Moving westward in France, minor names which belong in the Grenache's dossier are Fitou, Corbières and Minervois. In the extreme Southwest it is blended into a fortified red wine mostly of only regional interest. The wine is called "Grand Roussillon," and in the tiny Côte Vermeille district, near the Mediterranean, is called Banyuls.

Other members of the Mediterranean community who cultivate the Grenache under similar scorching conditions are Morocco, Algeria, Tunisia and Isreal. The rugged island of Corsica also produces a share of Grenache, and, though none of its wines is absolutely irresistable, one in particular clearly deserves recognition. It is called "Patrimonio" and is, as one might suspect—a rosé.

In California the function of Grenache is not just important, but absolutely essential. Beyond the renown of its most pleasing rosés, what makes it basic to California wine is that which makes it indispensible in Europe—its ability to thrive in the hottest climates. Usually second only to the Carignane variety in tons crushed each year, it covers roughly 17,000 acres in the state. Most of these are found in the consistently broiled counties of Madera, Kern, Fresno, Stanislaus and San Joaquin. It is from here that the largest wineries and cooperatives are supplied with raw materials for the tremendous quantity of everyday red table wines which now find their way to wine drinkers across the country.

Yet over and above this monumental contribution which has made California's inexpensive everyday wines among the finest in the world, Grenache will always be remembered for its joyous contributions to all those successful picnics.

Petite Sirah

plate 25

Petite Sirah

Viticultural Profile:

This vine is quite productive but has only moderate vegetative vigor. Due to this contrast, the management of the vine's crop load is quite important. In better soils no more than six to eight tons per acre should be produced. On non-irrigated sites of California's coastal valleys, only about two-thirds this production should be anticipated, if high quality wines are expected.

The vine is semi-upright to trailing in growth. The foliage is dark russet green with deeply five-lobed leaves. The vine often has only sparse leaf cover and fruit sunburn can be a problem.

The clusters are medium-large conical with heavy shoulders. They are often winged to double in shape. The berries are short, oval and heavily pigmented. The fruit ripens in late mid-season and with early fall rains bunch rot can be a severe problem.

An elderly gentleman, whose job is the care of wines during wood aging at one Napa Valley facility, will immediately steer you over to one particular spot when he discovers you appreciate a solidly-made red wine. Flashing a huge grin, he nods toward a group of oak casks. "Bet it wouldn't hurt your feelings to go a round or two with this one."

The wine reposing in those barrels is Petite Sirah. And these words are an eloquent understatement of its status in the minds of those who live so closely with wine and who prefer hefty, full red wines. California winemakers have always thought highly of this once mysterious grape and its wine.

Now, thanks to the expertise of the University of California at Davis, it is known that California Petite Sirah is a variety distinct from the European Syrah—probably either a clonal selection of the latter, or a selection of another Rhone Valley variety called Duriff. While all three are unique from a viticultural perspective, there is an underlying stylistic similarity among the best wines made in the Old and New worlds. Both French Syrah and California Petite Sirah display an aroma reminiscent of black currants, and, some say, fresh pepper; both offer a color intensity approaching blackness. In addition to these shared trademarks, both are massive, burly, mouthfilling wines, bursting at the seams with tannin and fruit acids in their youth. At maturity, they are smooth and rich as silk tapestries.

As is so often true of other great wine grapes, the early history of the French Syrah comes to us through a fog of folklore, legend, and myth, among which one picks and chooses. One widely held explanation accounting for the arrival of the Syrah in its homeland of the Rhone Valley is that the Crusaders returned with it from Shiraz, Persia (hence, the name) sometime during the late

12th or early 13th century. Others believe it to have been planted by the Roman legions or even earlier by the Greeks.

Of all the French Rhone Valley's numerous vineyard districts planted entirely or partially to Syrah, three have emerged over time as prominent. Far to the north are two miles of a sun-baked ridge called the Côte-Rôtie (roasted slope), located on the west bank of the Rhone River. The wines from this small area are distinctively aromatic, reminiscent of black pepper associated with the Syrah, and they are often lightened and refined by the addition of as much as 20 percent Viognier, a local white wine variety. Wines from this district are marketed under the appellation of Côte-Rôtie; the production is limited for these much admired wines.

Just north of the ancient Papal city of Avignon are the 6,000 acres of Châteauneuf-du-Pape, a district whose highly-prized wines owe their renown at least partially to the Syrah grape. The prevailing winemaking philosophy in this region is to make blended wines which can be made from any combination of thirteen different, legally permitted varieties. Syrah is always used to provide color, flavor and backbone in these attractive and most plentiful of fine Rhone wines.

Finally, Syrah performs a solo in one prestigious Rhone district. The lordly wine from the rocky hill above the village of Tain L'Hermitage. Its name now carried on the majestic wines from this area derives from the story of Gaspard de Sterimberg, a Crusader who was so repulsed by the bloody atrocities of the

Albigensian religious war of 1224 that he withdrew to the hillside, built a small hermitage, and dedicated himself to God and winemaking. Whether this is simply legend or actual fact is uncertain. But renunciation of worldly things and dedication to wine are not incompatible acts, as every winemaker knows.

The fame of Hermitage wines reached a peak in the 19th century when they were considered the peers of the first growth Bordeaux and the finest Burgundies. Though no longer so highly thought of, Hermitage still commands respect for its unique character, a marriage of the _Syrah_ grape to this special climate, soil, and exposure.

Outside Europe, Australia is one of the few countries worthy of mention in connection with _Syrah_ cultivation. Australians believe themselves to be in possession of the actual French _Syrah_ vine, thereabouts called _Shiraz_ or _Hermitage_, which thrives particularly in the Hunter River area, Victoria and the Barossa Valley. Somewhat lighter than their French counterparts, these wines are remarkably clean, with admirable varietal character.

The American equivalent of the Syrah, whatever variety it turns out to be, is not to be found clinging to any stylistic apronstrings, be they European, Australian or some other. The so-called "Petite" Sirah has benefited mightily from the innovative wind which has blown through California's wine country in the last few years, and brought new faces, daring ideas and fresh promises with it. Fifteen or twenty years ago, _Petite Sirah_ was considered only a "blending grape", usable for its pigments and tannin. Its production for varietal wines was not taken up until the Sixties, when it was still something of a lunatic fringe idea. Once established, however, those efforts yeilded constant and stunning improvements.

While the early pioneers of Petite Sirah in the Livermore, Santa Clara, and Napa Valleys were once making wines occasionally too tannic and heavy-handed, today there are many Petite Sirah wines offering excellent balance and enticing aromas and flavors resulting from refined vinification and aging techniques.

In the early days, this variety was planted indiscriminately; in today's market, there are vigorous, long-lasting Petite Sirahs, born of carefully chosen micro-climates and more exacting viticultural practices. The future looks dazzling for this variety in California; the one remaining chore is to seek out a more appropriate name than "petite" anything for this giant among red wine varieties.

Nebbiolo

plate 26

Nebbiolo

<u>Viticultural Profile</u>:

Nebbiolo is a variety of moderate vigor and productivity. It requires careful, but somewhat less-severe pruning in order to insure dependable crops. Although it grows only to a very limited extent in California, it should produce in the range of five to seven tons per acre.

The vine has deep green foliage with semi-upright to trailing shoot growth. The medium to small leaves, very deeply five- to seven-lobed, give the vine an open appearance.

The clusters are medium-large in size, cylindrical to long-conical and occasionally winged.

The berry is short-oval in shape and often lacks full pigmentation at the pedicel, which accounts for the low color of its wines when grown in warmer California climates.

The quality image of most Italian wines in America has never been spectacular. But for all implicit and explicit criticisms leveled at it, Italian wine does have its places, its times, its marvels. These are modest miracles, to be sure. Few would compare even the very best of them with the efforts of Château Lafite-Rothschild or Romanée-Conti, just as one doesn't compare Buicks with Bentleys.

In another sense, however, the discovery of some of these good, but less recognized bottlings can be as rewarding as the enjoyment of a much-acclaimed wine. Coming upon something done uniquely and well always creates a new perspective, a fresh appreciation. Among all of the Italian grape varieties, the two offering the greatest of these rewards to those open to them are undisputably the Nebbiolo and the Muscato di Canelli (see Muscat blanc).

The Nebbiolo's place is the verdant hillsides of northwest Italy, chiefly the Valle d'Aosta, the Novara Hills, central Piedmont and the Valtellina of Lombardy. Native to the region, the variety has gradually found its way, as great wine grapes will, to those specific locations best suited to its temperament.

Its time: probably the mild Italian autumn; the mornings when the Nebbiolo's namesake, the gentle Piedmontese fog (nebbia), spills onto the slopes like thick cream covering the berries, and growers smile in anticipation of a fine harvest.

The wines of these four major northern production areas have come under the strict viticultural laws of the Denominazione di Origine Controllata in the years between 1967 and 1971, though the producers' pride in their wines had in many cases previously matched or surpassed those specifications.

Their dedication obviously extends beyond some legal necessity. The common ideal and theme they share is a classical one: towering, magnificent reds which strike up a hearty exchange with game, red meats, perhaps a ripe Gorgonzola cheese. Wines which linger, warm and complete, on the palate and in memory. Though they share a bitter tannic, surly youth and a tawny, luscious nature in old age, each variation of place and method stands as a singular expression.

The Valle d'Aosta knows Nebbiolo as the Picoutener or Pugnet, which yields the medium-bodied Carema, and a similar wine granted its denominazione in 1971, Donnaz. Though less hefty than most of their relatives, these have taken on a silky, refined quality over time, probably from their alpine locations at the 3,000 foot level.

To the east, in the Novara Hills, Nebbiolo is called the Spanna. Here it gives us the powerhouse of flavor and body called Gattinara and Spanna, as well as their near equal, Ghemme. All three benefit immesurably from twelve to fifteen years of judicious cellering. Carefully-made lighter wines are also respected in these parts, most notably Sizzano, Voca, Lessona, and Fara. These are given over to blending and rarely use more than 60 percent Nebbiolo.

The central Piedmont district is the heartland of the finest Italian wines, and produces Nebbiolo's best known quality showpiece—Barolo. This is a tar-like, ungainly thing in youth, but after two years in wood and several years in the bottle, becomes a wonder. With an almost freakish intensity of scent—a rich, spicy autumnal smell—its flavor contains gentle suggestions of mushrooms and olives.

The lesser, lighter Nebbiolo wine, _Barbaresco_, is named for the town northeast of Barolo, while the more general wine appellation _Nebbiolo_, granted in 1970, represents the lightest of the Piedmont offerings. Even these are far from featherweight; several years of bottle aging is recommended.

The Valtellina, in the Lombardy District, one of the northernmost of Italy's wine regions, cultivates the Nebbiolo under the name _Chiavennasca_. Most of its clean, sturdy, claret-like wines, roughly 90 percent Nebbiolo, are shipped to Switzerland, though in recent years the United States has begun to awaken to their virtues. The outstanding wines here carry five traditional place-names: _Inferno_, _Sassella_, _Valgella_, _Grigioni_ and _Grumello_. It is said that Inferno is the weightiest and Grumello the lightest of all, but the old-time professional here will tell you that one who is not a native is hardpressed to distinguish among them. Believe him! The difference is in half-tones, if that.

In California, since even small-scale experiments with Nebbiolo have been few, it is difficult to assess its potential. Expert opinion is divided on the subject of suitability. Some insist the variety would yield a feature-less cipher of a wine if grown in fertile soils, while others say we simply have to do some more looking; we have to find that fog-bound north coast hillside which can coax the Nebbiolo's beauty into a new form, recognizable but new, mindful of tradition yet a pioneering effort nonetheless.

We like to think those seekers have a point.

Tinta Madeira

plate 27

Tinta Madeira

Viticultural Profile:

Tinta Madeira has proven well-adapted both to California's cooler and warmer growing regions. Naturally, it must be harvested late in the cooler regions, but when planted on good soils in the San Joaquin Valley, this grape can produce from 6 to 8 tons per acre of quality fruit.

The buds of Tinta Madiera are handsomely fruitful; the berries are long ovals of jet black, medium-sized, with thick but tender skins. Mature clusters are medium in size, broad-conical, often winged, and occasionally contain small green undeveloped berries. Usually they are well-filled to compact. Leaves are generally medium-large, three- to five-lobed and distinctly tomentose on the lower surfaces. Trailing shoots give the vine a low-growing, semi-prostrate appearance. This growth habit suggests avoidance of head-training which may expose the top of the vine to excessive sunshine, causing sunburning and raisining of the fruit.

Tinta Madeira is temperamental: when clusters are too compact, as they often are, they are prone to bunch rot—which may be reduced by judicious irrigation and cluster-thinning. In warm growing districts, the fruit matures early. In cooler regions, the berries are small, but even when harvested late, they arrive at wineries in surprisingly good condition. It is easy to hand harvest, but also may be machine harvested with fair success.

As its name indicates, the Tinta Madeira is believed to be native to the Madeira archipelago. At one time it was called Tinta de Madeira, a name which seems more explicitly indicative of its origin. It is a member of the Tinta family, a large clan prized for its capability for contributing rich, intense color to fortified dessert wines. To some extent, it is still cultivated in Madeira, and it plays a minor role in the production of Oporto wines from Portugal.

The fortunes of Tinta Madeira have ridden upon the vagaries of demand for Madeira wines. Fate has been exceptionally unkind during the last hundred years or so. But in the late 18th and early 19th Centuries, Madeira wines were held in quite high esteem on the Continent, in Great Britain and in colonial America. George Washington and Thomas Jefferson were both enthusiastic admirers of the silky character of Madeira wines—which they imported in 110-gallon pipes, or casks, shipped directly from Madeira. The Madeira islands, located off the west coast of Africa, were excluded from the normal trade restrictions and embargos under British rule. Madeira parties were popular and fashionable forms of entertaining and afforded the beginnings of many exclusive early American social clubs.

Disaster, in the form of phylloxera, the devastating plant louse, overtook the vineyards of Madeira in the late 1800s and the formerly brilliant wines were never again able to recapture their earlier prestige. Rather curiously, Maderia wines derive their unique "rancio" character by a method called "baking," meaning that the fermented wine is gently heated before it is fortified with brandy to achieve the desired alcohol content.

Professor Eugene W. Hilgard, of the University of California, Berkeley, in his courageous pioneering efforts to improve the quality of California wines, studied the Tinta Madeira closely during the nine years from 1884 to 1893.

Among his conclusions, he recommended Tinta Madeira for production of sweet dessert wines: "It has a smoothness and roundness of flavor which makes it more suitable for this purpose . . . and can be recommended for planting as a port grape." While he had held a preliminary opinion that the grape lacked acidity, his extensive follow-up investigations convinced him to grant Tinta Madeira his unqualified recommendation for cultivation in the warmer regions of California.

Obviously, somebody listened. As of now, there are over 1200 acres of Tinta Madeira in California, a substantial if not staggering amount. The acreage is concentrated in the warm San Joaquin valley counties of Fresno and Madera, adding a little luster to the faded facets of this variety. It is enjoying, so to speak, its just desserts—in the production of fine dessert wines. Tinta Maderia does lack tannin: made into table wine, it would yield an early-maturing light, sweet red wine with a tart flavor.

At this stage of the game, there is small demand for such a wine. On the other hand, when it comes to California ports, Tinta Madeira makes the best of them.

The consumption of California dessert wines has declined with the continued upward surge of table wines. But increased plantings of Tinta Madeira clearly indicate that California port producers are attempting to improve the quality of their products. Good color, fine productivity and the ability to develop high sugar content in warm regions overshadow the easily-avoided disadvantages of occasional bunch rot and raising.

Like sherries, most port wines are blends of different varieties and various harvests. In the Douro region of Portugal where the true port ("Porto") originated, the Touriga and Souzão reign as the most important quality varieties. Yet because it is somewhat deficient in color, Touriga calls for assistance from colleagues like Tinta Madeira and Souzão. Darker ports, such as Ruby Port and the occasional but marvelous vintage ports declared by shippers, owe at least some of their richness of color and depth to Tinta Madeira.

A close cousin, Tinta Cão, also grows in Portugal, but it lacks the intense color of its more spectacular relative. Vintage Ports and Ruby Ports provide two of the finest gustatory experiences in the world of wine, eulogizing the importance of Tinta Madeira.

The uncertain political climate of today's Portugal and the decline of Madeira's enological glories make it necessary for wine lovers to look to California as the source of fine ports in the future. The day may be closer at hand than we think: already one small port producer has demonstrated serious intent by winning widespread acclaim for his blended port and his Tinta Madeira "varietal" port; and a larger premium wine producer in Monterey County is making a magnificent port from the Souzão variety. Other large "premium" wineries are constantly striving to improve port-making methods.

As a specialty grape congruent to the development of great port-type wines, Tinta Madeira has long since earned its niche in the grape Hall of Fame. So long as this world shall be subject to the wrath of the storm, so also shall there by need for a good port to leeward.

Souzão

plate 28

Souzão

Viticultural Profile:

As a vigorous and moderately productive vine, the Souzão, in good sites, is capable of yielding between 6 to 8 tons per acre. In California's Central Valley, it has proven to be extremely fruitful when short or spur-pruned.

Souzão shoots grow semi-upright to upright. Leaves are deeply lobed, usually with three, and occassionally with five lobes. Thick in texture, they are wooly-white with tomentum on their lower surfaces. The clusters are medium-sized, cylindrical at times shouldered in configuration, and have a tendency to become compact when grown on very fertile, irrigated soils, which leads to problems with rotting.

Medium-sized and round in shape, the Souzão berries have an intense pigmentation, giving them a deep, bluish-black tint. At maturity, the profuse pigments will diffuse from the skin of the berries into their pulp, creating a distincitve pink or even at times a red hue. Its color intensity along with its easy adaptation to warmer climates make the Souzão a highly recommended grape for California's warm inland valleys. But it ripens very early and a tendency toward raisining is one of its primary liabilities.

Believed to have originated in Portugal centuries ago, the Souzão has been performing full service ever since in the production of one of the world's more fabled fortified wines, port. Made in an area _within_ a forty mile range from the town of Oporto, Port is a wondrous medley of as many as thirty different grape varieties and generally a blend of different vintages skillfully fused by craftsmen who create three basic styles: _Ruby_ (rich and full-bodied), _Tawny_ (light and drier) and, occasionally, _Vintage Port_, only made in exceptional years. Because many wines labeled "Port" have been made outside of Portugal in recent years, the name of the product made in Portugal has been altered to "Porto" to distinguish it from the others.

Essentially a blended wine, port, like claret and champagne gradually evolved over centuries. The English were the prime movers behind its destiny. To the English, port became the national beverage, as evidenced by the preponderance of English names in the list of many famous port shipping firms today. Enjoying a glass of Porto by the fireside after dinner is as English as Westminster Abbey. One suspects the cold clime of England may account for the popularity of port, but it also may be that this civilized beverage fit ever so nicely into the tradition of gracious living.

In the early 18th century when the English were denied the wine of France due to international discord, Portugal was seen as the immediate stopgap for imported wines. But to the refined English palates, Portuguese table wines were harsh and barely palatable. Thus, some enterprising seacaptain, now long forgotten, determined to improve his trade by adding some brandy to Portugese wines, for stability and appeal. Perhaps this is merely an explanation after the fact; yet it does explain in simple terms that port is sweet red wine brought up to higher alcohol levels by the addition of brandy.

Our founding fathers, Thomas Jefferson and James Madison, among others, were very fond of port wines, which they normally purchased in pipes, or large casks, to be placed in their cellars for entertaining. Unfortunately, there aren't many other noble associations between Port and the United States. Both before and after Prohibition, something labeled "California Port" was produced in large quantities, but the quality, to be charitable, was mediocre and the varieties were not the same. Port, say the experts, is a most difficult wine type to make, moreso than table wines.

The poor quality of "port" production in America didn't go unnoticed by those watchdogs of wine quality: the researchers from the University of California at Davis. In 1939, several experts from Davis toured the world's vineyards to collect information on how to improve the sweet dessert wines in America. They also collected many grape varieties along the way. One that made the return voyage with them to begin a new life in the Davis Experimental vineyards was the Souzão. But the grape first had to prove itself worthy in the California climate by undergoing years of vineyard testing and sensory evaluations.

The initial prognosis as well as the follow-up studies were most encouraging for the future of Souzão in the bright sunshine of the Golden State. World-famous enologist, Dr. Maynard Amerine, recommended the Souzão in 1955 for both its high color and fine natural acidity. Later studies singled out its intense color which, they reported, is one of its "most attractive features for the producer of red sweet wines." Again it was Dr. Amerine who studied fortified wines made from Souzão and concluded they ranked high "mainly because of their fruity flavors." When compared to several other grapes for port-type wines, "Souzão appears to be the most generally useful," concluded Dr. Amerine.

On paper, Souzão seemed destined to become a large favorite, except that the timing was off. The American consumers were beginning to drink table wines more than dessert wines. The eventual wine boom of the late 1960's and early 1970's was not much of a boon for producers of port. Nor did it enhance specialized grapes like Souzão which only increased over the last ten years by about 100 acres, bringing the grand total in California to 250 acres. While the figure is less than staggering, almost all of the Souzão is located in ideal sites along the warm Central Valley.

Though the quantity of port wine production has been drastically reduced recently, the quality has steadily been on the upsurge, since only those committed to quality continued plugging away. Many have experimented with blending Souzão with Tinta Madeira or other grapes to make more traditional port wines.

California can claim a small winery that specializes in ports and another larger one that introduced a variety labeled "Souzão Port," much admired by aficianados for its lovely fruity flavors and remarkable aging potential. These quite frankly are harbingers of better things to come, both for port wines in general and for the future status of the Souzão grape.

Also, a renewed interest in dessert wines seems likely to follow naturally from an appreciation of table wines with meals and as an integral part of gracious living. After a normal enough cultural lag, wine lovers will crave a port wine before the meal as an aperitif, or after, as a grand finale to a delightful dining experience. As wine consciousness continues to expand in America it will eventually encompass all dessert wines, including ports. With this expected revival on the horizon, California ports should once again rise in popularity, only this time one of the propelling forces should be none other than that historic, invaluable grape, the Souzão, a favorite of all skilled port blenders world-wide.

Concord

plate 29

Concord

Viticultural Profile:

This eastern giant, presumed of the *Vitis labrusca* species, is native to North America, east of the Allegheny Mountains. Although a strong growing variety, it is only moderately productive: on good soils—it prefers deep, gravelly, well-drained localities—the vine will yield six to ten tons per acre, and about one-half this amount in clay soils. It performs best in areas blessed with frequent summer rains and high relative humidity.

The Concord vine has a drooping appearance, resulting from a distinctly trailing shoot growth which benefits from a "double curtain" prunning/training system. Leaves are large, entire to moderately three-lobed (which is typical of *labruscas*) and leathery rough in texture. Upper leaf surface is dark green; the anterior side is whitish with profuse, dense tomentum. These features make the Concord leaf virtually unmistakable.

Concord clusters are small, loose to well-filled, often winged, containing from 25 to 40 large, round, blue-black (or purple-black) berries. Fruit is typified by the labrusca "slip-skin," with a soft, juicy layer immediately beneath, and a distinct, sharp aromatic character at maturity.

This vine is quite hardy: it can withstand winter temperatures as low as minus fifteen degrees Fahrenheit. In upstate New York, the Concord ripens toward the end of September or early October.

The reasoning student of American wine history cannot avoid a certain admiration for the Concord—if for no other consideration than its obvious link to viniana in America. It was the first grape to inspire colonial American growers; it provided the original impetus to winegrowing and hybridization. In less than a year after its introduction, please remember, its culture had spread halfway across the continent. In 1865, it was awarded the Horace Greeley Prize as the "best grape for general cultivation." Like the founders of this nation, the Concord was—and is—highly regarded for its offspring, which are numerous. Its virility is monumental, having begotten an uncounted number of descendants—both pure-and cross-bred. Its role in American wine culture is seminal, indeed.

Depending upon the ethnic legend you prefer, Columbian, Ericsonian (or according to more recent discoveries, Carthaginian, Tarsishian or Phoenician), whoever first set foot upon these shores discovered profusely growing wild grapevines. They flourished from Maine to Florida, but even from earliest recollections, the settlers—Europeans for the most part, who knew something about grapes and wines—realized that these "wild" grapes were not the same as those cultivated in Europe for table wines. Consequently, after simmering down for a hundred years or so, the colonial gentlemen aspired to import European wine varieties with a view toward bringing a touch of cultural nicety to this virgin land. To their despair, they discovered that _vinifera_ vines either would not grow at all in the high summer humidity and extreme winter cold of our Eastern seaboard, or, even where the vines managed to survive, the fruit refused to mature properly, being literally attacked by summer rots and various fungi.

Pioneers, conditioned by raw nature and the annoying foibles of His Majesty King George, were not prone to surrender their pride to an unresponsive grapevine. Thus, _circa_ 1800, some of the more determined former colonials turned their attention to the possibility of wrenching some kind of wine—for better or for worse—out of the native vines. In the southern regions—Georgia and South Carolina—the Isabella variety, another _Vitis labrusca_, grew handsomely, matured, and made an almost-passable wine. When transported north, it managed to survive New England winters; it ripened, but not to a degree that would be regarded—anywhere else in the world—as eminently suitable for winemaking. For the following half-century, the Isabella was the only grape of importance grown in New England, and anyone with a garden plot had a few vines.

Come 1843, one Ephraim Bull—who should be enshrined in an American Hall of Viticultural Fame—planted a handful of seeds from a native vine which had performed well in his home town, Concord, Massachusetts. A few years later, one of Mr. Bull's neighbors, who appears to have known something about such things, pronounced Bull's grapes better than Isabella. With such flattery and encouragement, the intrepid Mr. Bull presented his grape before the Massachusetts Horticultural Society, where it created a sensation. With due modesty and deference, Bull forfeited the opportunity to name the grape after himself, (for which we are forever in his debt!) and called it the Concord, further enriching the legend of that historic little city. Bull assumed his grape was some sort of hybrid: and repeated examinations over the years indicates the parentage of Concord remains obscure, but we can state with certainty that one of its parents, at least, was a wild labrusca vine.

Bull was energetic, restless and self-taught, a man of true Yankee ingenuity who accomplished what he set out to do: develop a grapevine able to produce mature fruit and survive the agonies of New England winter. He never became wealthy, but the Concord served him well. In his garden, he originated several other seedling grapevines—most of which have been forgotten. But the Concord lives on, much to his credit.

The Concord grape, says Philip Wagner, well-known author and vineyardist, "is good to look at, suitable for jam, and agreeable to eat out of hand. But it is not a satisfactory wine grape." Well, three out of four isn't bad. But in a world where it must become wine, the 'soul of the grape,' some say the Concord comes up short on soul. Yet it certainly doesn't lack heart.

Nor does it lack popularity. In the states of New York, Michigan and Washington, Concord is the leading commercial variety. Further, critics should know that about 85 percent of all plantings outside California consist of this variety. The flavor of Concord wine—as well as all other edibles and potables produced from this grape—is called "foxy," a term very likely based upon Aesop's fable, The Fox and the Grapes. It is the flavor all Americans associate with grape juice and grandma's grape preserves; it may be of passing interest that this precious flavor is created by an ester called methyl anthranilate, which is not found in vinifera varieties.

Admittedly, Concord does not make a subtle wine: bear in mind, however, that beginning wine drinkers are not seeking subtlety. The taste for wine is an acquired one, much as is a taste for martinis, olives or spinach.

For commercial wine, Concord seldom develops sufficient sugar, averaging around 14 to 16 degrees brix—well below that maturity desired for wine grapes. Consequently producers usually "ameliorate," or add sugar or grape concentrates in order to make stable wines meeting minimal legal alcohol standards.

"Elasticity" might be the word describing the Concord: it is fruitful, hardy, adaptable, disease-resistant, early maturing, and it survives in cold climates. Those who proclaim that the Concord's popularity impedes progress in quality winemaking in the eastern United States—and their arguments are well-supported—may be overlooking the fact that the wine boom of the 1960's was initiated by the invention of "Pop wines," such as Cold Duck and its _genre_, much of which was made from Concord grapes. And it is undeniable that many Americans were introduced to the joys of the vine through Pop wines.

There is a move today for table wines to be a blend of East and West wherein eastern Concord wines are blended with wines grown in California. Wines bearing the simple "American" appellation are usually blends of eastern _labruscas_ and west coast _vinifera_, properly publicized as 'the best of both worlds.' The concept was first advanced and inaugurated by Captain Paul Garrett, an early captain of the American wine industry before Prohibition. The Concord today is frequently used as a base for sparkling wines, often blended with French-hybrid wines.

Concord's early and continuing contribution to viticulture in America must, indeed, place it among the great wine grapes.

Carnelian

plate 30

Carnelian

Viticultural Profile:

Carnelian is a vigorous, productive vine with semi-upright growth. It fruits dependably when spur-pruned, and is capable of bearing ten to twelve tons per acre in the interior valleys. Its leaf is large, providing good protection for the clusters against sunburn. It has an undulated surface, is three-lobed and completely glabrous above and below.

Clusters are large, compact to very compact; however, bunch-rot is not a problem. They are short-conical and occasionally winged.

Berries are medium in size, slightly ellipsoidal to spherical in shape. The skin is thick, blue-black in color, with a heavy bloom.

The most striking thing about the history of the Carnelian variety is certainly its brevity. Its character is difficult to summon up. Only twenty-five years old, and only now entering into commercial use, one cannot call upon many experiences, past performances, traditions, or even the reader's experiences with wines from the variety in question.

We are left with little more than the baby book of this infant. And possibly a few anecdotes from the nursury.

Carnelian shares this characteristic with many other hybridized varieties under study at the Department of Enology and Viticulture, University of California at Davis. These new vines, among which Carnelian is now a relative old-timer, are under the constant scrutiny of their originator, Dr. Harold P. Olmo, the renowned geneticist, who hybridized the Emerald Riesling, the Ruby Cabernet, the Carmine and other varieties.

All are part of the constant effort by Dr. Olmo and his colleagues to find new combinations of varietal characteristics which will be more ideally suited to California's warm and sunny summer climate. Through them, it is hoped that the quality level of the state's bulk wines, already considered by many to be the world's best, will be raised still higher.

The Carnelian was hybridized with an eye to the fact that most of the grapes for bulk wines come from the Central Valley area, where two of the most-planted dry-red wine varieties are the Carignane and the Grenache. They have remained predominant largely because of their ability to thrive and produce big crops in that climate; the former makes relatively featureless coarse wine, while the wine from the latter although very fruity, lacks color and staying power.

The geneology of Carnelian can be traced back to 1936, at which time Dr. Olmo crossed Cabernet Sauvignon and Carignane to produce Ruby Cabernet. At the same time, a distinctly different sister hybrid was produced from this crossing. However, it was found to be self-sterile and required cross-pollination. It made wine which was very light and fast-maturing, and remained known only by its test number: F2-7. In 1949, during the course of more experimental crossbreeding, the F2-7 was hybridized with Grenache, and Carnelian was born.

The vine gave first fruit in 1954, and primary samples were promising enough to warrant the planting of experimental plots. These were realized in 1961 with locations in Fresno, Lodi, and Modesto, the last of these producing the first quantities of sample wine in 1966.

After exhaustive evaluation, the consensus was very positive. The overwhelming majority of samples were rated above average commercial quality by two panels—one from the University and one from the recently dissolved Wine Advisory Board, a California industry-supported marketing organization well-tuned to the American palate.

The wines resemble Pinot noir in many ways; they are very fruity, and have quite excellent acidity. Some samples which are eight years old are still improving in quality.

Also interesting to note is the variety's versatility—it is capable of producing fresh, light-bodied and flavorful rosé wines.

Biographical Sketches

Tim Ramey

The photographer and son of author Bern Ramey. Tim, one of the brightest young midwest professionals, is Director of photography with Don Deforest Associates in Elmhurst, Illinois, a suburb of Chicago. Tim was born into a wine-producing family and is acquainted with every phase of grape growing and winemaking. After graduating with Honors as a math major, Tim first became interested in photography as a hobby. His work has appeared in numerous leading U.S. magazines and has earned him national recognition in the field of creative advertising photography.

All photographs reproduced here were taken by Tim Ramey at the University of California, Davis research vineyards. To capture each grape cluster and its parts at their maximum maturity, the shootings and re-shootings took place over a three-year-span (1973 to 1976). The clusters and leaves on their canes were transferred from the vine immediately to the studio in the early morning hours and, from there, rapidly to the film. Immense care was taken to preserve the "bloom" on the grapes and to keep the leaves fresh, so that these photographs are true-to-life.

Tim shot each cluster in precisely the same manner—lit from the side and below with the help of a light table. The light was diffused through a translucent material as the quartz lights used would have been too harsh. A two-and-a-quarter by two-and-a-quarter Hasselblad camera was used in conjunction with a normal lens and a small extension tube, in order to position the camera as close as possible to the grape clusters. Nothing mechanical was done to improve the appearance of the clusters and their leaves.

Dr. Lloyd Lider

Lloyd Lider is Professor of Viticulture at the University of California, Davis, in the Department of Viticulture and Enology. It was Dr. Lider who personally hand-picked the clusters of each variety and gently transported them to the studio. Through his vast viticultural knowledge, he located the clusters that truly represented what the average picker would find at optimum harvesting conditions. The clusters were taken from the University's experimental vineyards where almost every known grape variety is grown.

Additionally, Dr. Lider was an invaluable wellspring of knowledge in the writing and compilation of each grape's profile, style, history, world-wide growth, and potential. Dr. Lider collaborated in the research and helped edit numerous drafts of each article.

Born and raised on a vineyard farm some 30 miles from Davis, Dr. Lider cultivated an early interest in grape growing through this childhood experience. In 1951 he was granted the Ph.D. in Genetics from Davis, and accepted a teaching position there, specializing in the research of grape rootstocks, vine pruning, and trellis studies. Dr. Lider is responsible for the Grape Varieties course taken by all viticultural students at U.C. Davis. Author of numerous published studies, Dr. Lider is also one of the co-authors of the second edition of the definitive text, _General Viticulture_, with Professors Winkler, James A. Cook, and W. Mark Kliewer. His studies and lecturing have taken him to almost every wine country in the world.

Bern C. Ramey

Bern Ramey, who many call the wine industry's Renaissance Man, has been successfully involved in just about every aspect of the wine field. Born in Toledo, Ohio, Ramey graduated from the University of California and Ohio State University, as a major in Greek and Music. He completed the University of California, Davis course in Enology and Viticulture in 1946, and later planted and grew the first French-American hybrids in Illinois where he founded a Champagne winery. Between 1947-1963, Mr. Ramey was wine sales manager for "21" Brands, Inc., and joined Browne Vintners as national sales manager, wine imports, in 1970. He is now a Vice-President of Browne Vintners, a Division of Joseph E. Seagram & Sons, Inc.

A busy lecturer and writer on wine, Ramey is a charter member of the American Society of Enologists, a lifetime member of the International Wine and Food Society, and associated with numerous other wine organizations.

He has also been active in the wine education and appreciation fields. Ramey put together the first Wine Record Album in 1964, edited _Wine Illustrated_, a quarterly publication, and authored the comprehensive and popular _Pocket Dictionary of Wines_. _The World Book Encyclopedia_ in its editions from 1974-77 contains an extensive essay on the history, production methods, and social and cultural aspects of wine, written by Bern Ramey. His business and his studies have taken him over much of the civilized world (and to some parts not so civilized).

As a member of _Who's Who in American Colleges and Universities_, Bern Ramey is a firm believer in education, the aesthetics of wine, and the efficacy of the written word. In _The Great Wine Grapes_, all three beliefs manifest themselves in every page.

Glossary
Essential Parts of the Vine

Berry

Apex	The lower or tip end of the berry.
Bloom	A thin wax-like layer covering the skin of the berry.
Lenticels	Small dots or openings on the skin.
Oblate	Spherical shaped with the ends flattened much like a pumpkin.
Ovoid	Egg shaped.
Slip-skin	Characteristic of *Vitis labrusca* berries; the pulp and seeds are separated from the skin by a juicy layer.
Stylar scar	A scar at the berry's apex left by the style of the flower.

Cane

Branch	A lateral development of the vegetative shoot.
Cane	A matured shoot containing fruitful buds along its axis.
Internode	The wood of the shoots or canes between two nodes.
Node	The place on the shoots or canes where leaves and buds arise.
Spur	A cane cut back to a short basal stub; usually retaining 2 to 4 nodes.

Cluster

Conical	A cluster shaped with upper shoulders and elongated apex.
Cylindrical	An elongated cluster lacking shoulders.
Globular	Short or nearly round shape of a cluster.
Pedicel	A small stem by which the berry is attached to the cluster.
Peduncle	The stem by which the cluster is joined to the cane.
Rachis	The main stem or branching framework of the cluster.

Shouldered	A cluster shape with one or more distinct branches closely attached to the main stem or peduncle.
Winged	A cluster with two separate, distinct parts attached at the main stem or peduncle.

Leaf

Basal veins	The main veins of the basal lobes at the petiolar sinus.
Convex	A leaf shape with the outer edges turned downward.
Entire	A leaf having no lobes.
Glabrous	Having very few or no hairs on the leaf surface.
Lobe	The rounded or angular projection of a leaf margin.
Petiole	The stem or leaf stalk which attaches the leaf blade to the shoot.
Petiolar sinus	The sinus formed by the basal leaf lobes at the petiolar attachment.
Serrate	Having numerous distinct teeth on the leaf margin.
Sinus	The depression in the leaf blade margin between adjoining lobes.
Teeth	Small angular or rounded indentations of the leaf margin.
Tomentose	Having hairs on the surface of the leaf.
Tomentum	The hairs on the leaf surface which may be single upright hairs, woolly white, or dense downy covering.
Veins	The ribs forming the interconnected framework of the leaf.

Shoot

Shoot	The current season's succulent top growth of the vine containing both the leaves and the fruit clusters.
Tendril	A modified cluster which gives physical support to the shoot by coiling around objects it contacts.
Trailing	A vine shape created by drooping or downward growing shoots.
Upright	A vine shape created by sturdy, vertical rising shoots.

Glossary

General Terms

Ampelography — The descriptive study and evaluation of grape varieties.

Botrytis Cinerea — The benign mold or fungus which, under certain climatic conditions and in certain districts, forms on the grape's skin, pierces it late in the growing season, and gives an enriched flavor and sugar concentration to the desiccated, shrivelled berries. Called pourriture noble (literally "noble rot") in France, and Edelfäule in Germany.

Clone — A group of vines (plants) originating from a single individual and reproduced by vegetative means, such as by cuttings or grafts. The unique characteristics of a single vine can be perpetuated by clonal propagation.

Concentrate — Grape juice elevated in sugar content by evaporating off water; used as an additive to low-sugar musts.

Fortify — To add brandy to increase a wine's alcohol content.

French Hybrids — Varieties of grapes developed by European nurseries by hybridizing European (Vitis vinifera) and American (Vitis rupestus, Vitis riparia, Vitis labrusca, etc.) species to produce phylloxera resistant, mildew tolerant vines.

Generic — A class or categorical description of a wine type, e.g., "Chablis," "Burgundy," "Rhine," etc. Once applied to wines made only within the clearly defined European boundaries, such wine-type names have passed into the public domain and are used by several other wine countries. They bear little or no resemblance to the original, authentic European models.

Must — Unfermented juice of the grape after crushing or pressing.

Mutation — A gene or chromosome change in vegetative cells which, following propagation, may lead to a permanent change in the clone. Some grape varieties show frequent clonal mutations, e.g., Pinot noir.

Phylloxera	The grape root louse, an aphid-like insect, which devastated the vineyards of the world during the late 1800's.
Pruning	The removal of living canes, shoots, leaves, and other vegetative parts of the vine. An annual vineyard practice which shapes the vine and establishes an optimum balance between leaves and fruit.
	Spur pruning (short) — A severe reduction in fruitful buds retained on two or three basel bud units (Canes); used with large clustered varieties.
	Cane pruning (long) — Practice by which twelve to fifteen bud pruning units are retained on canes; used with small clustered varieties and those low in bud fruitfulness.
Training	The arrangement of the vine on the supporting trellis to give a well-proportioned, easily managed vine for the production of quality fruit.
	Head training — A vine shape with the arms bearing the fruiting units arranged around a central head.
	Cordon training — A vine shape with the fruiting units arranged uniformly along permanent horizontal arms.
Varietal	A classification of wine by which wine is named after the predominant grape variety used to make it. Varietal nomenclature was instituted by California vintners shortly after Repeal and is now widely used in Alsace and other European wine districts.
Vitis Labrusca	A species of grapevine said to be native to North America.
Vitis Vinifera	The species of grapevines that includes all of the native European vines.
Vigor	The quality or condition that is expressed in the rate of growth of vegetative parts of the vine.